BALTIMORE A PORTRAIT

Published and Distributed by:

IMAGE PUBLISHING, LTD.

IMAGE PUBLISHING, LTD.

1411 Hollins Street/Union Square

301 • 566-1222   Baltimore, Maryland 21223   301 • 624-5253

Call or write for sales information.

For direct orders please send your name, address and a check or money order to the above address.
Hard bound books: $29.95 each plus $2.00 postage each.

Library of Congress Catalog Card Number: 82-91142 (Hard Cover)

ISBN 0-911897-00-3 (Hard Cover)

First Printing 1983. Second Printing 1984. Third Printing 1985.

Design, layout and editing by David Miller
Text by Dennis N. McClellan
Photo typesetting by S. Robert Gottesman of ABC Typography.
Printing, color separations and binding by DAI NIPPON PRINTING CO., LTD., Tokyo, Japan.

I would like to dedicate this book to my parents, (Ruth Dora Miller and Charles John Edward Miller), for their love, friendship and patience.
Thank you!
Roger Miller

I would like to thank everyone who had a part in this project. Specifically I would like to thank the following people:

I would like to thank Mayor William Donald Schaefer for his invaluable assistance.

A very special thanks to Bill Boucher and everyone (especially Grace Petty, Jim Vipond and Ann Boucher) at William Boucher, III and Associates for all their time and efforts on *Baltimore A Portrait*. "Expect A Miracle" is the sign which sits on Bill Boucher's desk and is the reality which comes out of his office.

I would also like to thank Dennis McClellan of CentraBank for his belief in *Baltimore A Portrait* and for his effort which made it a reality.

For their efforts and belief in this project I would like to thank everyone at CentraBank, particularly Lee Boatwright, Mike Glump and Paul Gettings.

For efforts and encouragement far beyond the call of duty I would like to thank Sarah R. Hecht. Without her organization and ability to decipher my writing this credit might have ended up illegible and on page 50.

For their friendly and professional assistance on this project and numerous others, I would like to thank ARTOGRAPHER LABORATORIES, INC., Baltimore, MD, and ATLANTIC PHOTO SUPPLY CO., INC., Baltimore, MD.

A special thanks to all the people and businesses in Baltimore. Without their assistance, this book would not have been possible.

Roger Miller

BALTIMORE A PORTRAIT
Photography By Roger Miller

Text By Dennis N. McClellan

Foreword By William Donald Schaefer, Mayor

Design, Editing By David Miller

CONTENTS

FOREWORD

By William Donald Schaefer, Mayor

The Baltimore Renaissance is very real and very important. It shows that an old city can be a vital, attractive place to live and work. Certainly today's Baltimore has proved its vitality, its attractiveness. Each year millions of visitors come to Baltimore to enjoy our Inner Harbor, our museums, our sports teams, our places of historic interest.

Over the past few years Baltimore's Renaissance has been responsible for thousands, perhaps even millions, of words. Students from grade school to university have used it as the topic of term papers. National magazines have sent their best writers to cover it. Newspapers have turned out thousands of column inches about it.

But if you really want to know Baltimore, you must go into our neighborhoods, for they are our strength. For many visitors, our Inner Harbor, with its modern pavilions, superb aquarium and other attractions stands as a shining example of the renovation and rebirth of old cities. And it is impressive. But it is not enough, because a city is people, not buildings.

And you find Baltimore's people in Baltimore's neighborhoods. Baltimore has been described as a city made up of small towns, and to a great extent, the description is true. Ask a Baltimorean where he's from and he'll say "Highlandtown," or "Park Heights" or "Bolton Hill" or "Cherry Hill" or "Charles Village" or "Reservoir Hill" or "Forest Park" or "Pigtown." Neighborhoods. Places where we live with pride.

At one time, not too many years ago, Baltimore's neighborhoods were threatened. Families were moving to the green grass of the suburbs, speculators were taking over housing, deterioration had set in and people doubted there was a future for our City.

But today there is a new spirit in Baltimore, in our neighborhoods. The children of families who had moved to the suburbs are moving back to town. It makes good economic sense. Housing costs less in the City and there are mortgage plans to help families get their first house. Commuting becomes a simple bus ride. Stores are around the corner or down the block - not five miles away amid a sea of parking lots.

Today it is not unusual to see entire blocks undergoing renovation. Young people with more energy than money know they can invest that energy wisely in Baltimore row homes. Older people are drawn by the knowledge that sound, distinguished, housing is to be found under the layer of deterioration. And people who have invested so much effort, so much money, so much love in a house are going to do what they can to make the rest of the neighborhood a fine place in which to live. They join neighbors who never doubted Baltimore is a fine place in which to live.

The words "neighbor" and "neighborhood" still mean something in Baltimore. Our people look out for one another. They are willing to watch a neighbor's house, run errands for a neighbor who is sick or handicapped, raise funds to give a neighbor's child a summer job.

In the following pages, Roger Miller has looked at Baltimore through the lens of his camera. He has examined how we live, how we work, how we study and how we entertain ourselves. He has captured our people, our buildings, our present and our past. And he has hinted at our future. All in all, the look has been loving.

WILLIAM DONALD SCHAEFER, Mayor

INTRODUCTION

Welcome to Baltimore A Portrait. This book is just that: a portrait, a collage of images, an artistic composition of impressions and feelings that emphasize the texture and pattern of a most unique subject — Baltimore.

Although this book takes a contemporary look at the new Baltimore, the Renaissance City, it is important that some historical background on the city be given. For to understand Baltimore today, it is valuable to know something about its past.

It most likely began with the arrival of the first tourist, John Smith, who is given credit for the discovery of the Patapsco River in 1608. He was impressed with the area and named the river he sailed, the Bolus. Well, the name of the river has changed, but the attraction of the land Smith mapped became quite a magnet for English and European settlers.

Following an act passed by the Assembly in Annapolis, several towns were created. These were sorely needed to market the products being grown by the increasing number of farmers and to serve as ports of entry. Today's Baltimore is actually the third town that was named for an Irish village and the Lord of the colony. The first, erected in Harford County, failed. The second, on the Eastern Shore, failed. It was the third and final venture that became a success and today continues the love affair.

A real bargain at 40 shillings an acre, the 60 acres that became Baltimore Town is now the site of modern, downtown Baltimore. From the very beginning it was important that the town become a successful port. The Jones Falls that ran along the eastern border of the town would play a big part in the future success of the community, as would the harbor created by the Patapsco.

Three competing communities merged over the years: Baltimore Town, Jones Town, and Fells Point. In 1796, the city of Baltimore was incorporated by the Maryland State Legislature. The port continued to grow and service a diverse product line. There was the tobacco that grew in the new state of Maryland and was popular in England and Europe. There was also an increasing demand for Pennsylvania wheat, Baltimore County iron and glass, refined sugar from the city of Baltimore, and the flour milled in Carroll and Howard Counties.

The first real census of 1800 found some 31,514 citizens living in the boom town. During the early years, Baltimore wanted to pay homage to George Washington. The military and political hero had visited the city many times, stopping at his favorite spot, the Fountain Inn on Light Street. Years after his death and through the use of funds raised by the sale of lottery tickets, the city dedicated a monument on a high spot in Howard's Woods to Washington. What a day! Some 20,000 people gathered for The ceremonies — five times the number that gathered on Federal Hill in 1788 to celebrate the ratification of the Federal Constitution. It is interesting to note that the monument was erected in Howard's Woods (considered a safe, rural location), because the city leaders were concerned that the tall column might prove dangerous and perhaps topple over on the populace.

It should be pointed out that just one year before the ceremony to dedicate the Washington shrine, the city of Baltimore was seeing another sort of fireworks over the harbor. The British, who had just ransacked the White House in Washington, had arrived on the shores of Baltimore with full intention of doing the same to the port city. Unaware that the city was prepared for such an attack, the British landed at North Point and tried to blow Fort McHenry out of the harbor. In short, the defense of the city was made possible by the likes of men like General John Sticker, General Sam Smith, and Colonel George Armistead. During the battle between the British fleet and the defenders of Fort McHenry, Francis Scott Key, a Georgetown lawyer and poet, who had made a futile effort to gain the release of a friend being held prisoner by the British, observed the bombardment and wrote the words of our National Anthem.

The 1820's were another important growth period for Baltimore. The National Road had opened to the West and connected the city and its port to the Ohio River. To compete with the Erie Canal, an innovative means of transportation was needed. In 1828, the city turned out to celebrate the laying of the cornerstone of the Baltimore & Ohio Railroad. The B & O was the first chartered railroad in America and by 1829 the first experimental locomotive, the Tom Thumb, was being built in Baltimore by a New York inventor, Peter Cooper. In 1830, a now-famous race was held between the Tom Thumb and a horse-drawn car; the locomotive broke down and the horse won. Nevertheless, railroads became the next step in the growth of Baltimore.

During the early 1830's, a young man came to the city, and spent a few years here producing some minor writings. Although he left before fame came his way, Baltimore has always felt close to Edgar Allen Poe and that affection continues to this day. Tourists and city dwellers visit his home on Amity Street and his grave in Westminster Presbyterian Churchyard.

The period of the Civil War was one of economic hardship for the region around Baltimore. As early as April 1861, the Union had reason to question the loyalty of the city, when a mob attacked troops of the 6th Massachusetts Infantry as it passed through on its way to Washington. The results brought martial law to Baltimore and eventually barrels of cannon, planted on Federal Hill by Union General Butler, directed right into the center of downtown. At the end of the war, the port resumed its commercial superiority.

Another important development occurred just after peace was secured. The

Peabody Institute opened its doors in October of 1866. This internationally known Institute has produced some of the finest musicians, directors and composers in the country and has been an important part of the cultural life of the city.

During the 1870's, a new sport became extremely popular with Baltimoreans: horse racing. Pimlico, a racetrack on the outskirts of the city, began holding meets in October of 1870. The feature race of the first meet was called the Dinner Party Stakes and was won by a colt named Preakness. Three years later, the first Preakness stakes was run. Today, The Preakness attracts thousands to its May event — the second leg of the Triple Crown.

The latter part of the nineteenth century was filled with events that proved that more and more people owed much to Baltimore and wanted to return something to the city. Johns Hopkins willed millions of dollars for the creation of a new hospital and university that both bear his name. Enoch Pratt provided funds for the building of the city's library system and for building facilities intended to make radically important changes in the care and treatment of the mentaly ill.

As the city entered the twentieth century, it was obvious that the port was thriving and the region had become a leading center for manufacturing and industry. However, just as the century was getting started, it appeared that maybe it was all coming to an end. In the early days of the new year (1904), a small fire started in a drygoods warehouse on what is now Redwood Street. Before the conflagration was over, most of the commercial area of downtown Baltimore was devastated. Although no lives were lost, the loss in property was estimated upwards of $150 million.

Reconstruction of the commercial center of town was immediate and swift. Within a year after the fire, the city was well on its way to a complete recovery. New piers and access roads made Baltimore a more planned and orderly city.

The years prior to World War I were productive and fast paced. Woodrow Wilson was nominated for the presidency at the Fifth Regiment Armory by the Democratic National Convention in 1912. Babe Ruth left the St. Mary's Industrial School and briefly joined the Baltimore baseball club prior to being sold to the Boston Red Sox. The Bromo-Seltzer Tower was erected in 1911, being the tallest building in Baltimore, with a revolving Bromo bottle on top. And in 1914, the U.S. Frigate Constellation returned to the port of Baltimore where she was built in 1797.

The city benefitted from the numerous outstanding citizens who had shared their lives, their time and energy for the betterment of Baltimore and the nation. Among these were James Cardinal Gibbons, the second American appointed to the post of cardinal by the Roman Catholic Church. Today, a popular high school bears his name and attracts both Catholic and non-Catholic students. There was Henry Walters, who upon his death willed his art collection, started by his father, William, and several million dollars to maintain the gallery which became a city art museum in 1931. There were popular writers of the day like Ogden Nash, whose comic verse became so famous and H. L. Mencken, the iconoclast of Union Square, who was famous for his quotes and hoaxes. It might be said that Mencken more or less wrote his own epitaph when he remarked: "If, after I depart this vale, you ever remember me and have thought to please my ghost, forgive some sinner and wink your eye at some homely girl."

The hustle and activity that came with the world wars brought additional prosperity to the region. Industry, such as steel, oil, ship building, and repair facilities grew during the period and created jobs. The end of World War II brought a boom in the housing market and a heavy demand for office space and commercial services that accompanied the boom. However, the city began to witness an exodus from the city by thousands of residents who began to seek suburban life. Baltimore also suffered economically from deterioration of its port facilities. Rather than sit back and let the city slide completely into decay, the Greater Baltimore Committee was organized and dedicated to the development of both the economic and cultural life of the city.

That mood which existed in the 1950's, that imagination, astute planning, and initial dedication, can be seen today in the results of over thirty years of hard work and effort on the part of thousands of recognizable and unknown names. The results can be seen today in the expansive Beltway that circles the city, the Jones Falls Expressway that serves as a major artery to and from the suburbs, the Charles Center complex of major downtown office space and residential facilities, the redevelopment of the port, the unbelievable restoration of the Inner Harbor and the creation of Harborplace, the World Trade Center, the National Aquarium, the Maryland Science Center, and the huge Convention Center.

The results were not seen overnight. That is obvious. What many people are also aware of is that much of what Baltimoreans have loved so long has existed for hundreds of years in an unspoiled way — even if restoration has played a strong part in their continued existence. For example, there is the Lexington Market that celebrated its 200th birthday in 1982. This popular gathering place has served the city throughout its long and often-trying growth periods. Today, in its expanded and modernized facilities, the market continues in its long tradition of serving up the freshest fish, meat and food products at the best prices in town. And then there is Fells Point, the birthplace of the U.S. Frigate Constellation. Today, Fells Point is the scene of home restoration, a real sense of history and its preservation. It is an area that offers some delightful restaurants and bars, and it gives the tourist or first-timer an opportunity to taste the flavor of what old Baltimore was like.

So, as you turn through the pages of this book, see the love affair that continues today in Baltimore. The things the city loves are all here: the Orioles, the new Meyerhoff Symphony Hall, the Baltimore Museum of Art, the Flag House, and the Inner Harbor. But most of all, witness the love affair between people and neighborhoods — between people and Baltimore. Baltimore is a product of its own history. And this book is dedicated to the Old and the New Baltimore.

INNER HARBOR

A feast for all the senses, Baltimore's Inner Harbor is an on-going festival. From early morning until the wee hours of the next day, visitors from all parts of the nation and around the world mix with natives who never seem to lose their enthusiasm for the city's centerpiece. The air is thick with the aroma of fresh-baked pastries, seafood from the Chesapeake Bay, Mexican specialties, a multitude of crepes and quiches, hot dogs and submarines, tempura, and Indian delights. Smell the fragrance of fresh-cut flowers, spices, herbs, and roasting coffee. Smell the excitement.

During a magnificent celebration in July of 1980, Harborplace was formally opened. The promenades have not been empty since. However, this was not always the case. The 3.2 acre site was once a mere portion of what had become a rotting and blighted wasteland. Although Baltimore had once been able to claim a significant position among the principal ports of the eighteenth and nineteenth centuries, this portion of the city's harbor had fallen on very bad times. To bring the harbor to its present condition and give back to the citizens of Baltimore a revitalized and magnetic center of activity, the city pulled together the very best minds and imaginations of both the public and private sectors.

The renaissance of downtown Baltimore, including the Inner Harbor began in 1956 with a gathering of the Greater Baltimore Committee and the Committee for Downtown. Over the years, a number of individuals have made significant contributions to the eventual success that today draws more than 18 million visitors a year: names like Mayors Thomas D'Alesandro, Jr., Theodore R. McKeldin, and William Donald Schaefer, William Boucher, III, and James Rouse stand out.

Today the dramatic turn of events can be seen as the culmination of years of dedicated efforts on the parts of many in the business community, local government and private life. The Charles Center-Inner Harbor Management, Inc., formed in 1964, became an outstanding model of public and private organization at its very best. It continues to work closely with the city and developers to produce results that will serve the citizens of Baltimore today and tomorrow.

In its first year of operation, Harborplace with its green-roofed pavilions and its neighbors — the National Aquarium, the Maryland Science Center, the U.S. Constellation, and the World Trade Center — combined to entertain more visitors than Disney World, produced an income of some $42 million, and provided jobs for nearly 2,500.

Walk the promenades, sit at an outdoor cafe, watch the mimes and magicians, enjoy a taco or scoop of locally made ice cream, stroll the deck of a ship built 166 years ago, or engage in an endless array of activities offered up by one of the most exciting places in the nation.

HARBORPLACE

A showplace that has drawn major acclaim from its critics and praise from all corners of the nations, Harborplace has sent a positive bolt of energy through the entire city. Costing an estimated $20 million, the project has more than lived up to the expectations of its strongest supporters and its planner, James Rouse.

The two glass encased, bi-level shopping and eating pavilions, offer the visitor over 140 shops and restaurants to choose from. Cards, dresses, hats; Italian food or crab cakes; a kite or a tee shirt — the selections are endless. Year round, this is an exciting place to experience Baltimore at its best.

Phillips

INNER HARBOR

Stroll the brick sidewalks of the Inner Harbor or cross any of the brightly colored, covered pedestrian bridges and one cannot help but notice that the harbor attracts thousands of people. The Inner Harbor Marina, a full-service facility for pleasure crafts of all sizes in some 160 slips, attracts thousands of boating enthusiasts each year.

PHILLIPS SEAFOOD RESTAURANT

You can experience the culinary delights of Maryland's Eastern Shore at the Inner Harbor Phillips Seafood Restaurant. Last year Phillips Restaurant in Harborplace was the fourth highest restaurant in the United States in gross sales. Phillips is still a family owned restaurant which was begun in Ocean City in 1957.

NATIONAL AQUARIUM

Walk past a 260,000 gallon pool that has contained dolphins and currently holds seals, wander among a dazzling display of aquatic life in their natural habitats, and enter the Rain Forest where brilliantly colored birds live among the lush vegetation. This paradise is located on Pier 3 and is known as the National Aquarium.

Designed by architect Peter Chermayeff, the educational showcase is one of the largest and most sophisticated aquariums in the country. It houses over 8,000 specimens of 600 different fish, birds, mammals, reptiles, amphibians, and invertebrates; and through a unique program, known as Aquadopt, people may adopt an animal of their choice for a period of one year — contributing to its care and feeding.

MARYLAND SCIENCE CENTER

On the West Shore of the Inner Harbor the curious will discover the world of the Maryland Science Center home of the Maryland Academy of Science — the second oldest institution of its kind in the United States. With exhibits that include geology, evolution and the Chesapeake Bay, one could spend an entire day enjoying the displays. The Davis Planetarium allows the adventurous to travel through space; and the K.I.D.S. Room allows preschoolers to discover science on their level of understanding.

WORLD TRADE CENTER

"The keystone of the Inner Harbor," as Mayor Schaefer tagged it. The World Trade Center was conceived more than 15 years ago by the Maryland Port Administration and is today the focal point for all maritime and international interest in the Mid-Atlantic region. Its unique pentagon design provides unobstructed viewing from any window of the 30-story structure. An observation deck on the 27th floor provides a bird's-eye view of downtown Baltimore and the beautiful harbor below.

HARBOR LIGHTS MUSIC FESTIVAL

In a 2,000-seat music pavilion on Pier 6, Baltimoreans can boast of having the largest structure of its kind in the country and a first-of-its-kind urban entertainment center. Throughout the summer a veritable collage of entertainment is featured: from Ella Fitzgerald to Gordon Lightfoot, from the Preservation Hall Jazz Band to Dave Brubeck, and the sounds of Glenn Miller.

PADDLE BOATS, USS TORSK, LIGHTSHIP CHESAPEAKE

The Inner Harbor offers a variety of water going vessels. For the young and young at heart, there are the ever popular paddle boats. A fun way to see the harbor from its best vantage point, paddle boats are the energetic's answer. For those that like their history with a salty flavor, there is the USS Torsk (SS423). This World War II submarine holds the distinction of having fired the very last shot in that war — a torpedo that sank a Japanese coastal defense frigate. Another floating piece of history is the Lightship Chesapeake on Pier 4. Built in 1930, she is listed on the National Register and remains one of the few fully operational lightships in existence. Both vessels are part of the Baltimore Maritime Museum.

PRIDE OF BALTIMORE

Whether docked at home or traveling the open sea toward a distant port, the Pride of Baltimore is the floating representative of the city's business community. Launched in 1977, she sails from Baltimore to other ports in the nation and world as did the clipper ships of the past.

U.S. FRIGATE CONSTELLATION

Launched in 1797 in Fell's Point, the Constellation is the oldest ship in the world continuously afloat. Today the scene of visiting school children and history buffs, this U.S. Navy frigate saw action in the War of 1812, against the Barbary pirates in North Africa, and sought out slave ships as flagship of the African squadron in 1859.

The John Eager Howard Room

ENTERTAINMENT & RECREATION

Something for everyone. . .It is a fair claim for Baltimore to make. Whatever the taste in food, drink, recreation, or entertainment, Baltimore can fill the need.

Some of the finest hotels in the United States have always been found in Baltimore. Ever since Charles Dickens praised the accommodations and food at Barnum's City Hotel and H. L. Mencken drank a fond farewell to alcoholic beverages at the beginning of Prohibition at the Rennert Hotel, Baltimore has had a long tradition of fine lodging establishments.

Today the city proudly boasts a new Hyatt Regency on the Inner Harbor, the popular Hilton complex, and the stately Belvedere Hotel. The future is bright with additional hotel construction, some nearly completed, that will enable the city to face the ever-increasing numbers of visitors and convention goers that will be arriving each year.

Baltimore has become a major convention center. Since its opening just four short years ago, the Baltimore Convention Center has seen a full schedule and received the praise of all who have utilized its facilities. The $50 million structure on the corner of Charles and Pratt Streets that covers over 400,000 square feet of exhibit space is just a stone's throw from the Inner Harbor. The two have combined to make the city an unbeatable package.

Visitors and Baltimoreans alike love good food. Without a doubt, food is one thing that Baltimore can provide — in any ethnic flavor, in any amount, at any price. The names of restaurants themselves are like fingerprints that undeniably identify the foods they serve: Olde Obrycki's Crab House, McGinn's, Great American Melting Pot, Trattoria Pettrucci, Jean Claude's Cafe, Schatzie's, Ikaros, Madrid Restaurante, Bamboo House, and The American Cafe. Take your choice, the selection is nearly endless. If you have a craving for crab in a way that only Baltimore offers, oysters, rockfish, or clams, if scampi, veal or homemade pastas are your desire, or if the taste of kataiffi, mou sou pork, or salmon with cucumber sauce is on your mind, the fine restaurants of old and new Baltimore await you.

Whether it is a noon-time concert in Hopkin's Place, a juggler performing for a crowd at Harborplace, a breathtaking ride at the City Fair, Baltimore knows how to enjoy itself. By day or by night, there is always some form of recreation or entertainment available to the interested. A full array of ethnic festivals offer great food and entertainment for the entire city on weekends throughout the summer. The famous City Fair is the paramount festival each year, bringing all neighborhoods together for one big party.

Look around and you cannot help but notice that this city knows how to enjoy itself. Take a closer look and you will see that a great many of those enjoying the recreational activities of Baltimore are visitors or guests. It is those happy visitors who take back to their hometowns and states the message that Baltimore is a great place to visit and to live. Today, more than ever, a statement by H. L. Mencken makes sense: "no literary tourist, however waspish he may have been about Washington, Niagara Falls, the prairies of the west, or even Boston and New York, ever gave Baltimore a bad notice."

HYATT REGENCY

With 500 rooms and 25 suites, the glass and steel Hyatt Regency opened its doors in 1981, offering the finest of accommodations to the visitor of Baltimore. An atmosphere of casual elegance prevails, enhanced by the proximity of the Inner Harbor. With numerous hubs of activity — including a rooftop restaurant which commands a sensational view of the Inner Harbor, a specialty restaurant set amid trees beside an indoor lake, and a full service restaurant with its own cascading waterfall. This spectacular hotel has a multi-lingual staff and can handle conferences of as many as 2,000. Inside the lobby, a six-story atrium greets new arrivals with its greenery and flowers.

THE BELVEDERE

Known to many as the "Grand Lady" of Charles Street, The Belvedere is Baltimore's renaissance hotel. Once entertaining such guests as Al Jolson and Enrico Caruso, this stately and elegant thirteen-story landmark today offers, in addition to rooms of old-world style and grace, culinary delights in the John Eager Howard Room. Here one can taste some of the finest dishes prepared in Baltimore, while surrounded by arched windows, high ceilings, chandeliers, velvet banquettes, fresh flowers, and music flowing from a baby grand piano. In addition guests may sample the menu of the Owl Bar, a nostalgic pub that dates back to 1904, and the delightful view of the city from The 13th Floor, a contemporary lounge with live jazz.

OMNI INTERNATIONAL HOTEL

Omni International Hotels has acquired the Baltimore Hilton. A renovation of 9.3 million dollars is planned to update all the rooms and facilities. With over 730 picturesque rooms and suites, the twin-towered Omni occupies an entire city block in downtown Baltimore. The original, North Tower was opened in 1967 and the complex was completed in 1974. Located within walking distance of the Inner Harbor, the Convention Center, and most center-city activities. The Omni offers its guests plush appointments, a gourmet restaurant, lounge, meeting and banquet facilities for up to 1,500.

The Brass Elephant

The Prime Rib

Miller Brothers

THE BRASS ELEPHANT, PRIME RIB, MILLER BROTHERS

Northern Italian cuisine is offered in the most comfortable of surroundings at The Brass Elephant, a meticulously restored 1861 townhouse. One of the more beautiful features of this multi-story restaurant is the stamped-metal ceilings. This restaurant is typical of the high degree of attention that is given to both menu and appointments in Baltimore's best dining places.

Opened in 1965, the Prime Rib specializes in American cuisine and offers "a little bit of Manhattan in Baltimore." With elegant prints and plush surroundings, this 130-seat restaurant is a popular gathering place for in-town celebrities.

Miller Brothers at the Hilton offers fine dining and elaborate meals that complement the exquisite dining rooms they are served in. With fresh flowers, mirrored and quilted walls, and an atmosphere of the sea, the restaurant is a Baltimore tradition that dates back to 1912.

Tio Pepe

Velleggia's

Tio Pepe

VELLEGGIA'S

Velleggia's is the oldest, original family-owned restaurant in Little Italy. Like its fine counterparts in this popular section of the city, it has been attracting customers from the surrounding areas of Baltimore for nearly fifty years. Originally known as Enrico's Friendly Tavern in the 1930's, this popular dining spot serves, among its varied offerings, a much-requested Saltimbocca and Calamari Marinara.

TIO PEPE

Always a top choice among Baltimoreans, Tio Pepe is an outstanding example of Spanish cuisine. A favorite spot for a romantic dinner, this whitewash-walled restaurant provides the perfect setting for enjoying the ambience of Andalusia in Baltimore.

Lexington Market

Culinary Arts Institute

Haussner's

CULINARY ARTS INSTITUTE, LEXINGTON MARKET

Baltimore's International Culinary Arts Institute got its start in 1972 at the Community College of Baltimore. Today, at its current location on South Gay Street, it is one of the few professional culinary schools emphasizing international and ethnic cooking.

For over 200 years the Lexington Market has been a favorite eating and shopping area, with a reputation for having the freshest food products in town.

HAUSSNER'S

Haussner's is as much an experience as it is a restaurant. Boasting the largest private art collection in the city, this Eastern Avenue dining spot also can brag about having the largest menu as well. Established in 1926, Haussner's offers sauerbraten, baked goods from its own bakery, potato dumplings, strawberry pie, and hundreds of selections. Serving some 2,000 meals each day, the staff has reached more than 200.

37

BALTIMORE CONVENTION CENTER

Since it opened in the summer of 1979, the Baltimore Convention Center has transformed the city into a nationally recognized location for trade shows and conventions of all types. The complex features four exhibit halls that can be divided into twenty six customized rooms for a total of 115,000 square feet. Its unique construction allows for two completely different activities to take place

simultaneously without interference or confusion. Dramatic architecture and good use of furnishings, plants and glass, plus the travertine marble sculpture by Henry Moore in the lobby all combine to make the Convention Center unique among all others.

Automobile shows, publisher's conventions, or political functions (such as the Carter-Reagan debate), the Convention Center has, by its own records, hosted groups of people 300 days out of a calendar year. The growth of Baltimore in the next few years will make this a most desirable location for any group.

BALTIMORE ZOO

In Druid Hill, on 150 wooded acres live nearly 1000 animals at the Baltimore Zoo. Open year round, the Zoo offers visitors an opportunity to see many animals in their natural settings: Masai lions and giraffes in a predator-prey, open-air exhibit, numerous endangered species that are being protected and sometimes bred, and the largest colony of black-footed penguins in the country. A focal point of the Zoo is the restored Rogers mansion house that serves as administrative headquarters. The old Boat Lake is home to more than eighteen species of waterfowl at the nation's third oldest zoo.

City Fair

City Fair

Ethnic Festivals

Ethnic Festivals

CITY FAIR, ETHNIC FESTIVALS

Held in September as it has since 1970, the City Fair has, as Hope Quakenbush put it, shown that Baltimore is not a melting pot, but a stew with many different ingredients. For three days at the Inner Harbor, the people of the city are the stars and neighborhoods are showcased. Recognized as the first and finest city fair in the nation, Baltimore's has served as the prototype for other cities to emulate.

Ethnic festivals have been taking place in Baltimore for more years than many

remember: the German festival being the oldest; it started 83 years ago. Held at Rash Field on week-ends, these fun-filled, food-filled festivals bring representatives of the city's unique neighborhoods and organizations together. American Indian, Afram, Polish, Estonian, Irish, the list goes on and on; and so does the fun and brotherhood.

PREAKNESS BALLOON RACE

Preakness Week has become as much a part of May as the famous race itself. Among the activities that take place preceding the Preakness Stakes at Pimlico Race Course and one of the more colorful, is the balloon race from Druid Hill park to the Eastern Shore over the Chesapeake Bay. Balloons contain about 40,000 to 85,000 cubic feet of heated air. To the winner goes a special trophy named after The Preakness.

THE BLOCK

The truth is that no city in the country has The Block or anything quite like it. This unique part of Baltimore-Americana is as brash as the eyes and ears tell you it is. Made famous by names like Fanny Belle Fleming (better known as Blaze Starr), "The Oasis," Little Egypt (whose show was closed by police), "The Gayety," Phil Silvers, and Moana the Jungle Queen, The Block has survived public indignation, world wars and the onslaught of endless Marines, sailors, conventioneers, and high school boys. Today it seems fair to say that The Block is as much a part of Baltimore as steamed crabs.

GIRARDS

Baltimore has always been a city that came alive after dark — especially in the forties and early fifties. During the seventies night life in Charm City saw a rebirth of activity with a variety of locations to select from: the Pimlico Hotel, The 13th Floor, Sweeney's (local home of the twist), O'Dells, and the Hippopotamus to name a few. Girard's on Cathedral Street has been declared the city's ultimate disco with both live and recorded music. As in many of the more popular places around town, the mood in music taste often dictates how quickly the sounds change at Girard's.

Fort McHenry

HISTORIC MONUMENTS

With the formal dedication of the cornerstone for the first monument in the country to George Washington in 1815, Baltimore was well on its way to earning its title as the "Monumental City." It is interesting that as one travels the city and reflects on all of the history that has taken place here, and considering all of the historic locations and buildings that have been lost to fire, flood, urban renewal, and in some cases, lack of concern, that so many valuable artifacts of the past have been preserved. All one has to do is open their eyes; history is there, staring right back.

Just three years after thousands of cheering citizens jammed onto the hillside of Howard's Woods to watch the beginnings of what was to become the Washington Monument, a lieutenant-colonel of the Swedish fleet, one Baron von Klinkowstrom, visited the site and viewed the incomplete monument and declared it not very beautiful. However, as an example of how impossible it is to please everyone or predict the reactions of tourists, consider this opinion generated by Frances D'Arusmont, a well known writer of the early nineteenth century, while she and her friends were on a walking tour of Baltimore: "Heated with fatigue and want of rest, we suddenly came upon a spacious fountain, where the clear cold water, gushing fresh from the spring, ran gurgling over a channelled floor of marble . . . at the foot of a little hill, sprinkled with trees, upon whose top is a noble column, raised to Washington. . .Ascending to it, we saw this beautiful little city spread at our feet; its roofs and intermingling trees shining in the morning sun, the shipping basin, crowded round the point; while, in the distance, the vast waters of the Chesapeake . . . stretched beyond the more cultivated precincts of the young city."

Fort McHenry, sitting majestically at the entrance to Baltimore harbor, has witnessed the passing of adventuresome clippers as they carried American merchandise around the world and the onslaught of naval war vessels. In 1814, after raiding Washington and burning the Capitol and the White House, British forces launched both a land and naval attack on the city. Under the leadership of men like General Sam Smith, General John Stricker and Colonel George Armistead, the invaders were repulsed and the city saved.

The flag that flew over Fort McHenry during the fierce fighting is now on display at the Smithsonian in Washington; the home of the woman who created the symbol of unity has been preserved as a national shrine on East Pratt Street. Today, at the corners of Calvert and Fayette Streets, you can see the city's recognition to the men who fought to protect Baltimore in those threatening days. The Battle Monument cornerstone was laid in 1815 and September 12 has been known as "Old Defenders Day" ever since.

The bold scheme that became the Baltimore and Ohio Railroad got its start here in the mid-1820's and by 1829 the first railroad locomotive, the experimental, "Tom Thumb" was ready for competition — against a horse. Although the horse won, the B & O went on to have a glorious history. Today that history is preserved for all to see and experience first hand at the B & O Railroad Museum at Pratt and Poppleton Streets.

It was in June of 1816 that Rembrandt Peale, famous for his portraits of wealthy Americans, shocked his guests who were visiting his small museum with a demonstration of illumination by carbureted-hydrogen gas. As a direct result of this, the city fathers granted permission to the Gas Light Company of Baltimore to light the streets of the city, thus creating the first gas-light company in the nation. The Peale Museum today is a wonderful place to discover Baltimore, with its exhibits on the "rowhouse," the Peale Family, and its galleries of art and artifacts related to the city.

The Carroll and Mount Clare Mansions, the impressive Engineers Club (housed in the Farrett-Jacobs Mansion), and the Evergreen House are excellent examples of the splendor and grandeur that was part of Baltimore's history. Each is a monument to the architecture of a period and to the families who built them. Today they provide a window on a time now gone, but preserved.

Travel the streets of this city and you cannot help but see the statues, homes and monuments erected by, sculpted by, and lived in by people now gone. The wonderful fact is that these tributes are here for us to appreciate today.

WASHINGTON MONUMENT

With a 39-gun salute, a symbol of the young country's age, amidst handsome paintings that depicted the "Father of His Country," with a stirring rendition of Yankee Doodle, followed by a 100-gun salute, and fireworks that evening, the Washington Monument cornerstone was officially laid on July 4, 1815. The area now known as Mount Vernon Place was then Howard's Woods and quite rural, being a full mile from the harbor. Some 20,000 strong gathered that day to

celebrate what was to become the very first formal monument to the nation's military and political leader. Completed in 1829 and paid for with funds raised by public lottery, the monument stands 178 feet tall. The 160 foot shaft of native marble was designed by Robert Mills; the handsome figure of Washington was carved by Causici and depicts the Commander-in-Chief as he resigned his commission. Today the site is a hub of activity that is surrounded by beautiful parks, the statues of other famous men (like the equestrian sculpture of the French officer and personal friend of Washington's, Lafayette), and a neighborhood that was once one of the most elegant residential sections of Baltimore. For the energetic, a climb to the top of the monument is a good physical test and provides a great view of the city.

FORT MCHENRY

Once the scene of fierce combat between the naval vessels of the British fleet and the defenders of Baltimore, Fort McHenry became a part of America's history during a 25-hour period that inspired Francis Scott Key to pen the words to the "Star-Spangled Banner." That infamous day in September of 1814 found Key, a lawyer and poet, the prisoner of the British. He watched from the deck of the Minden as Congreve rockets were launched toward the Fort and later wrote of their "red glare" as they bombarded the defenders.

Originally built as Fort Whetstone in 1776, the purpose of its construction was the defense of the entrance to Baltimore harbor. Later, in 1798 the name was changed to honor the Secretary of War, James McHenry, a resident of the city. Today the Fort is a popular part of any tour of the city. Evening Tattoo ceremonies are held regularly by a military band. And on June 14 of each year, the National Flag Day Committee holds its "Pause for the Pledge" ceremonies at the Fort.

STAR-SPANGLED BANNER FLAG HOUSE

On the corners of Albemarle and Pratt Streets stands the home of Mary Pickersgil, creator of the huge, 30 x 40 foot flag that flew over the troops defending Fort McHenry during the War of 1812. Interestingly, Mary was born in 1776 and her mother Rebecca Flower, had made the first unofficial flag of the U.S.A., Great Union for George Washington. Furnished in the Federal period, the home has an excellent collection of early American art and framing the house is a gracious garden.

CARROLL MANSION

Built in the year 1812, when the young American nation had just gone to war with England, the Carroll Mansion was the idea of Charles Carroll. Located at 800 East Lombard, the mansion is decorated with rich period antiques.

Carroll was the last surviving member of the delegation of rebellious colonists who signed the Declaration of Independence. He was the founder of the Baltimore and Ohio Railroad, and by the late 1700's he held the distinction of being the wealthiest man in the country. The mansion was occupied by Charles Carroll during the last ten years of his life.

MOUNT CLARE MANSION

A beautiful place to visit at any time of the year, the Mount Clare mansion takes on a particularly festive air during the Christmas holidays. This Georgian style plantation was constructed between 1754 and 1769 and is the oldest home in the city of Baltimore. Mount Clare served as the home of Charles Carroll the Barrister, a cousin of Charles Carroll of Carrollton and signer of the Declaration of Independence. Today the mansion may be visited and viewed as if Mr. Carroll were still living there and about to entertain his good friend John Adams.

ENGINEER'S CLUB

Located at number seven Mount Vernon Place in the Farrett-Jacobs Mansion since 1962 is the Engineering Society of Baltimore. Restored to its original splendor, the Victorian mansion is most magnificent. Once the home of Mrs. Henry Barton Jacobs, the very prominent social opinion maker of Mount Vernon Place, the residence contains forty rooms with such splendid features as a theatre, an art gallery, and library. Its famous supper room was known as the Hall of Mirrors. And the mansion has its own conservatory. Although it required four separate homes to produce the mansion, the thirty-two year project put to work two of the leading architects of the day, John Russell Pope and Stanford White.

EVERGREEN HOUSE

At 4545 North Charles Street, Evergreen House is a beautiful mid-19th century mansion. Maintained amid manicured and lush grounds, the mansion houses numerous art treasures. In this accessible home, the visitor finds that Evergreen House is more than a mere museum. Here one can view the Dufy collection of fine paintings, elegant pieces of Tiffany, the rare book collections of the Hopkins and Garrett families, and see examples of Japanese carvings known as Netsuke. This elegant carriage house is decorated in the styles common to the 1930's and 1940's, interspersed with antiques and art pieces of earlier times.

MARYLAND HISTORICAL SOCIETY

Founded in 1844, the Maryland Historical Society is located on Monument Street, just off Mount Vernon Place. The ever-growing collections of the Society are preserved as the irreplaceable treasure they are and maintained for future generations to enjoy and study. These collections include furnishings, porcelain and silver collections, toys once enjoyed by children of an earlier Maryland, clothing and costumes, tools, priceless paintings, military and maritime artifacts, jewelry, clocks, a library of more than 80,000 volumes, pamphlets, bound newspapers, and more than 2,000,000 original letters, pieces of sheet music and manuscripts. Its publication, the *Maryland Historical Magazine,* has received national acclaim.

BALTIMORE ARTS TOWER

Known on sight to most Baltimoreans, the Baltimore Arts Tower is more commonly known as the Bromo Seltzer Tower. Once bearing a towering, 51-foot reproduction of a blue Bromo Seltzer bottle, the structure, now void of its giant bottle, is the home of the Mayor's Advisory Commission on Arts and Culture. Built in 1911 as corporate headquarters for the Emerson Drug Company, the tower is a reproduction of the Palazzo Vecchio Tower in Florence, Italy.

SHOT TOWER

Shot used for ammunition during the 17th century was made by dropping molten lead from the top of tall towers through sieves and into cold water vats below. The process was quite universal. However, Baltimore's shot tower is unique in that it was completed in just six months and was completed without using any outside scaffolding. The tower was in use until 1892, sixty four years after its construction. There is only one other like it in the Western hemisphere.

POE HOUSE

Used by the master writer and poet between 1832 and 1835, the Edgar Allan Poe House is located at 203 Amity Street. The home has on display books and paintings belonging to the author. In a garret chamber in the building Poe did produce some works. Poe, his wife and mother-in-law are buried nearby in the Westminster Churchyard at Fayette and Greene Streets.

BABE RUTH HOUSE

Just recently renovated as a museum, Babe Ruth's birthplace is now dedicated to memorabilia about the Bambino, the Baltimore Orioles and Maryland's baseball heritage. Located at 216 Emory Street, the home features the upper floor room where George Herman Ruth was born on February 6, 1895.

Peale Museum

Mencken Home

WAR MEMORIAL PLAZA, PEALE MUSEUM

A focus for a number of city-sponsored activities, the War Memorial Building and Plaza cover two city blocks that stretch in front of City Hall. A favorite spot for lunchtime entertainment, this renovated area is popular during the warm weather months.

Distinguished as the first building in this country (1814), to be built strictly as a museum. Selected as the first City Hall, and serving as the first black primary school in Baltimore, the Peale Museum was renovated and reopened in 1981 as a museum dedicated to the city. The museum was founded by Rembrandt Peale the famous American portrait painter.

MENCKEN HOME

The home of Baltimore's most famous iconoclast, H. L. Mencken, is now open to the public at 1524 Hollins Street in Union Square. It was this home that Mencken selected following the death of his wife Sarah, and it was here that he lived until his death at age 75 in 1956.

BALTIMORE STREETCAR MUSEUM

Since the last streetcars were taken from Baltimore streets in 1965, the Streetcar Museum is the only place in the city where one can experience the joy of riding one of these unique conveyances. Located on Falls Road, a mile of reconstructed track enables the visitor to relive an era now gone. Displays and exhibits, plus a film on the subject, takes you back to a period in travel that began in 1859.

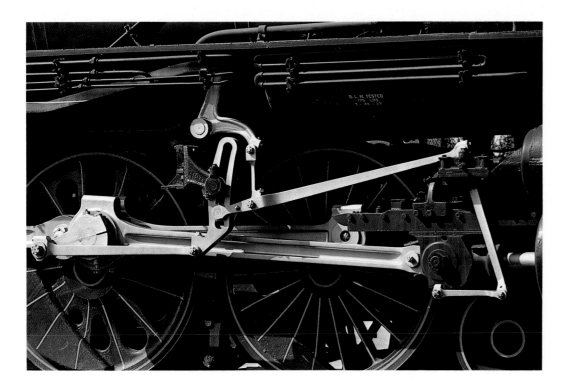

B & O RAILROAD MUSEUM

When Charles Carroll broke ground for the B & O Railroad on July 4, 1828 he said that he considered what he was doing second only to signing the Declaration of Independence, "if second to that." Today visitors to the Museum can relive the days of steam engines. Here one can see a reproduction of the nation's first railroad depot built in 1830 (Mt. Clare Station). In the round house built in 1884, one can see original tracks and the wooden turntable which have been preserved. In addition to elaborate parlour cars, there are model trains that can be manipulated and an exciting collection of artifacts from an era of railroading now only history. Perhaps its most interesting display piece is "Tom Thumb," the nation's first locomotive.

Edmondson Village

NEIGHBORHOODS

In his work, *The Eclipse of Community,* Maurice Stein wrote, "People need to believe in the value of the communities in which they live, the goals that they seek, and the satisfaction they receive." Take a look at any Baltimore community and use this yardstick to measure its people; chances are that they will measure up.

Baltimore is as diverse in its neighborhoods as it is in the subs offered by any of the city's delicatessens. Its neighborhoods are old, new, restored, under restoration, preserved, and gone. But one thing is sure for those neighborhoods that have survived transition: they are alive.

With characteristics that are uniquely their own, each of Baltimore's neighborhood communities has something to offer that is found in no other part of the city. You cannot really appreciate the diversity by merely listening to others talk; descriptions lack one vital quality: you cannot touch, feel or taste them. Baltimore needs to be explored and experienced.

There are portions of the city that have been functioning since the 1600's; there are other sections that did not develop until the years after World War I. Some neighborhoods have a strong marine and nautical flavor, others are as inner-city as those found in most major American cities, and still others suggest to the visitor that they are in some rural environment.

Whatever the neighborhood, there is one common denominator, one feeling that permeates: pride. Baltimore is a city alive with a spirit of renaissance and an indisputable desire to survive. Look into the neighborhoods and you will see a defiance that has kept some alive through the worst of economic and natural destruction. Look at others and you will see a vision that brings people together in a mutual search for a future.

Part of the effort to keep Baltimore's neighborhoods alive can be seen in the various projects undertaken in recent years. During the 1950's a handful of people understood the importance of conserving the best of the city's properties. Today, it is no longer necessary to consider throwing oneself in front of a road grader or bulldozer to save a piece of history.

Through the combined efforts of city government and private individuals, urban homesteading became a reality. The idea was not necessarily new, but the approach was. So-called "dollar houses" went on the market and blighted areas came back to life. Today the idea has enveloped the city and many important older neighborhoods are being reclaimed.

To insure that interest is stimulated in Baltimore neighborhoods, some have made efforts to, more or less, sell themselves to others by providing educational walks that will point out the richness of the local history and hopefully gain an appreciation for the diversity of the community. Such walks were provided in recent years by Ridgely's Delight, Hampden and Union Square.

Another effort to strengthen communities is the Baltimore Neighborhood Resource Bank, designed to solicit non-cash donations from businesses. In turn these resources will be allocated to communities undergoing improvements.

However, when all is said and done, the main force that makes neighborhoods great in Baltimore is the people. Neighborhoods are not buildings and history. Neighborhoods are communities of people that believe in the value of what they have, that seek a better life through common goals, and recognize the satisfaction that can be received from their joint efforts.

Look through these pages and see the pride and satisfaction that comes from a spirit of community in Baltimore.

MOUNT VERNON

Inspiring fountains and splendid parks, tree-lined walkways and sculpture by distinguished artists are hallmarks of Mount Vernon Place, site of the annual Flower Mart. It was on land initially donated by John Eager Howard, hero of the Battle of Cowpens during the American Revolution, once known as Howard's Woods, that this charming corner of Baltimore was created. Dominated by its centerpiece, the Washington Monument; Mount Vernon affords a view of what many of the city's leading families called home: the Walters, Jacobs, Peabodys, the Pattersons, and the Garretts (whose home became the first location of the Baltimore Museum of Art).

In elegant mansions and impressive brownstone surroundings, in homes whose architecture was influenced by French and Italian revivalists, contemporary British dwellings, and the likes of Stanford White, lifestyles were far different from

those of Baltimoreans in general. Across from the homes were small parks, laid out with care as early as the late 1820's. Today's residents include small shops and restaurants, as well as the sculptural works of Grenier ("Boy and Turtle"), Berge ("Sea Urchin"), and Barye ("War and Peace" and "Seated Lion"). Some of the older buildings survive: the Walters Art Gallery, the Peabody Conservatory of Music, the Engineers Club, the Mount Vernon Methodist Church (constructed in 1872 on the site of the home in which Francis Scott Key died), and the 22-room mansion known as the Harry Gladding House.

Walk the sidewalks of Mount Vernon, feel the cobblestones under your feet in the balustrade, try to ignore the parked cars and the sounds of a modern city, listen to splashing water from nearby fountains, and you will find that much of the ambience of a bygone era survives in this unique Baltimore neighborhood.

MOUNT WASHINGTON

Situated on and among the rolling hills west of what was Washingtonville, Mount Washington served as a country retreat for numerous Baltimore families of wealth during the middle and late nineteenth century. Today many of the homes built during the Victorian period and early twentieth century still dot the hillsides, connected by winding streets. Shopping is a major attraction to those who come to visit the popular community, and much of this area has been rebuilt over the years as a result of the flooding of the Jones Falls.

Currently only a few minutes from downtown Baltimore, Mount Washington was originally linked to the city by the Baltimore and Susquehanna Railroad. The rails are gone, but the flavor of this once-rural land is still visible in its preserved homes, its still-wooded landscape, and atmosphere of country living.

Coldspring

Coldspring

Cross Keys

Cross Keys

COLDSPRING

Contemporary Baltimore faces new challenges daily. One challenge is to house her people and to provide unique and stimulating surroundings at the same time. Enter Coldspring Newtown. Designed by the internationally-acclaimed architect, Moshe Safdie, and built to house 10,000 people, this modern answer to housing is an outstanding example of planning. Residents are offered a variety of housing options that are both innovative and aesthetic.

CROSS KEYS

With its name stemming from a village that once stood in the nearby area, and much of its construction taking place on what was once a golf course for the Baltimore Country Club, Cross Keys is an example of the work of master planner James Rouse. With its own style of sophistication, Cross Keys offers Baltimore a most interesting community that blends a variety of housing environments and the concepts of ownership and rental alongside each other.

STIRLING STREET

It was called "urban homesteading," but it meant rebirth. Stirling Street, northeast of the center of Baltimore, just a block west of the Old Town Mall, was the first urban community project of its type in the nation. Here, twenty-five homes that had been abandoned and left to rot were resurrected through a unique concept known as the "dollar house" project. The result had a rippling effect throughout the city.

FEDERAL HILL, SETON HILL, FELLS POINT

Once called John Smith's Hill, Federal Hill received its new name in 1788 following a huge celebration to mark the ratification of the Federal constitution that was attended by some 4,000. The Hill area has seen some interesting history as a signal tower, marine observatory, and a battery for Union cannon during the Civil War. General Benjamin Butler trained his guns on the city and threatened to place his first shot, if needed to quell any trouble, into the Maryland Club

Federal Hill

Federal Hill

Seton Hill

Fells Point

which was thought to be a hotbed for Southern sympathizers. Today the area is active with restoration projects that are bringing to life the 100 to 200 year old row houses that had once lost their dignity.

Settled in the early 1790's, Seton Hill takes its name from the first American-born saint, Elizabeth Ann Seton. Its history dates to an order of French priests who initially lived there. However, its future lies in the dedication of its preservationist residents.

Fells Point may be the most "changed" unchanged community in Baltimore. This multi-ethnic area is home to some 350 original structures dating back to the 1730's. Here maritime and shipping activities go hand-in-hand with rehabilitation, restoration and tourism. The home of the Constellation and Bertha's Mussels, Fells Point has something to offer everyone.

EAST BALTIMORE

East Baltimore is people. Even with a change in the population mix, the strengths that made the communities, that make up East Baltimore, have not been altered. Hard work, strong religious ties, a belief in family and friends, dedicated community organizations: all these are East Baltimore. From its famous hand-painted screens to its union halls, East Baltimore is a major part of what makes the entire city great.

Known as Hampstead Hill during the British attack of September 12 and 13, 1814, Patterson Park today is a busy city park that provides a variety of athletic activities for local residents. Numerous buildings from the last century dot the park, including the Chinese-style observatory known as the "Pagoda."

Otterbein

Hampden

Otterbein

Ridgely's Delight

OTTERBEIN, RIDGELY'S DELIGHT

South Baltimore showplace; that is what many see when they look at Otterbein. Staying as true as possible to the architecture of the 1780's as they could, urban pioneers moved into this once thriving community during the 1970's and brought with them a new lease on life for themselves and a residential area dealt a harsh trick by time and progress. Just a stone's throw from the Inner Harbor, Otterbein was transformed from a rotting eyesore into a success story of

rejuvenated Federal period homes and storefronts. An impressive example of the largest dollar homesteading projects in the United States, Otterbein is a living trip back into the eighteenth century.

Named for a plantation once owned by Charles Ridgely and paid for with the dowry brought by his wife (the daughter of John Eager Howard), Ridgely's Delight has experienced a vivid history. George Washington visited the

76

Hampden

HAMPDEN

In single homes of clapboard and shingle, in unpretentious brick rowhouses, and in millworker's homes built of stone from local quarries, this community has resisted time and economic changes to remain one of Baltimore's most resilient areas. Pride and a strong work ethic survive in this once world renowned mill town; such is the fundamental and distinctive qualities sought for the individuals honored by the annual "Hampden's Best Awards."

community from time to time; medical professionals constructed ornate rowhouses reflecting an Italian influence that differed from the existing Federal style, and commercial structures added their own influence on the area. Today, with the community zoned for residences only, Ridgely's Delight is well on its way to a new life under the movement toward restoration.

CHARLES VILLAGE

Steep tiled roofs, projecting bay windows, and stained-glass: these are just a few of the surviving architectural qualities to be found in Charles Village. Once known as Peabody Heights, it was this area north of the center of town that many sought to live. Close to the estates of some of Baltimore's most notable families — the summer home of Charles Carroll's son and the mansion of Mayor Samuel Brady to mention two — sprang up some of the first homes in what was called the "suburbs." The major structures of the area are the rowhouses, each as distinctive as the builder whose work reflected the trend of the day. Additional distinction was added to the area with the arrival of the Woman's College of Baltimore (now Goucher) and Johns Hopkins University. Today, Charles Village, renamed by activist Grace Darin, is a thriving area bustling with renovation and vitality.

BOLTON HILL

Rumor once held that anyone who was anyone lived in Bolton Hill. The rolls of the famous (F. Scott Fitzgerald, Gertrude Stein, and the Cone sisters) and not-so-famous that have and do live in this twenty block area are impressive. Strong wills and considerable expense have saved this elegant, tree-lined community of nineteenth century townhouses. Named for the 1805 estate of British merchant George Grundy, Bolton Hill was once described by Henry James as "the gem of the town."

A stroll through the streets of Bolton Hill is worth the time and can be like walking through a Victorian dream. One of the more charming attractions is Bolton Common, recognized by the American Institute of Architects for its design. Take a look; here are Baltimore traditions restored, maintained and thriving like no where else in the city.

Roland Park

Dickeyville

Roland Park

Dickeyville

ROLAND PARK

Set in a patchwork of individualistic homes that sit among well-manicured lawns and heavy vegetation and woods, Roland Park is today, as it was at its inception, well planned. One of the first planned communities in the nation, it holds the distinction of having the first shopping center in the country as well. Today the area reflects the heavy influence of landscape architect Frederick Law Olmstead, the creator of New York's Central Park.

DICKEYVILLE

Drive down the narrow streets that once took workers from their stone and clapboard houses to the nearby mills along the Gwynns Falls, and you take a trip back into history. Converted warehouses and restored frame homes that have survived both flood and fire now serve as the residences of a modern era. In marked contrast to the hustle and complexity of the city that surrounds it, Dickeyville provides an almost rural setting and a glimpse of what life was.

GUILFORD

Guilford can boast that some families have lived for more than three generations among the lush foliage that dots this post-World War I planned community. Created on an estate of the same name, once owned by A. S. Abell, this residential area set many standards now considered commonplace in newer communities: assessments for maintenance, subdivision planning for parks, and

local vigilance to prevent commercial intrusion.

One of the highlights of Guilford is Sherwood Gardens. Once the private effort of a single family, Sherwood Gardens today is recognized as the finest floral display in Baltimore. Through the efforts of the community itself, the Gardens are Guilford's gift to the city that cannot be duplicated.

Union Square

West Baltimore

Union Square

UNION SQUARE, WEST BALTIMORE

With debate still continuing about the origin of its name, Union Square is another of Baltimore's historical preservation districts that has seen great popularity in recent years. Dating back to the 1780's, this German and later Lithuanian neighborhood was the chosen site of H. L. Mencken's home. Today, through the efforts of the Union Square Association, restoration is encouraged and guided by rules established to protect the integrity of interiors, as well as the exteriors,

of homes that are as varied as Victorian, Georgian, and even Mexican-modern. The primary aim of the residents of Union Square is the creation of a Victorian village that is accessible by foot from the center of Baltimore.

West Baltimore is another cog in the ever-changing city that it serves. Edmondson Village, whose history dates from pre-revolutionary days and gained prominence as a shopping center, has been the victim of demographics and

82

West Baltimore

neglect. It has been through the efforts of its long-time residents (like Mayor William Donald Schaefer) and an attempt at balanced integration, along with renewed initiatives on the part of businesses that the spirit lives on in Edmondson Village.

Today West Baltimore is alive with activity and rejuvenation. Communities like Lafayette Square are attracting new residents who are interested in preserving the unique architectural appeal of this parcel donated to the city in 1856 by land developers. Harlem Park with its three-story brick and fieldstone houses is a restorationist's dream come true. West Arlington developed around the turn of the century and today is striving to preserve its original architectural character. And Walbrook, with its rich history dating back to 1669, is representative of the spirit that has affected the rest of Baltimore.

THE ARTS

To many of us, the word "art" might conjure up the idea of entertainment; such as a novel or motion picture, even a television show or concert or exhibition of paintings or prints because they offer a way to pass time in a pleasant way. However, the word "art" also implies a specific type of entertainment — one that is connected with beauty and creativity and involves some element of aesthetic satisfaction. The arts reflect the character of individuals and communities; they are an essential part of the humanity of a community. In this respect, Baltimore is fortunate to have a significant role to play as the home for some of the most outstanding art institutions in the nation.

The Baltimore Museum and Gallery of Fine Arts was built in 1814 by Rembrandt Peale, making it the oldest original museum structure in the nation. From such beginnings, Baltimore has grown and matured. Today the city offers a variety of galleries that serve the tastes of local patrons as well as those of distant cities. Among these are: C. Grimaldis Gallery and G. H. Dalsheimer Gallery on North Charles, Maryland Art Place at Market Place, Meredith Contemporary Arts on North Charles, Eleanor Abell Owen on Bellona, School #33 Art Center on Light, Unicorn Studio in Fells Point, and Tomlinson Craft Collection on North Charles.

Of course, the major attractions in Baltimore for art at its very best are the Baltimore Museum of Art and the Walters Art Gallery. The Walters, the older of the two (built in 1908), is home to one of the most comprehensive and renowned art collections in the world. Within its richly decorated rooms, the visitor can go from Egypt to Medieval Europe; the works of Daumier and Raphael share the walls along with Monet. It is a credit to the Walters family that modern Baltimore has such a wealth of important art to enjoy.

The Baltimore Museum of Art, after serving the city for many years and displaying some of the finest works in the world, opened a fantastic new wing on October 17, 1982. As part of its Inaugural Exhibition, four new galleries displayed works of four contemporary artists who had close ties to the state of Maryland and to the city of Baltimore. Among the artists in this exhibition were: Grace Hartigan, Anne Truitt, Morris Louis, and Clyfford Still. In addition to various other collections made available to the visitor, the world famous Cone Collection of largely French works of the early twentieth century were shown throughout the museum.

Baltimore has a rich heritage in schools of art. The Maryland Institute for the Promotion of the Mechanic Arts, which opened in the 1820's was the first of many schools to produce artisans. In addition to the Maryland Institute College of Art, Baltimore offers interested students opportunities at Towson State University, The Community College of Baltimore, Notre Dame College, Goucher College, Coppin State, Morgan State, and the University of Maryland, Baltimore County.

Another art form that has found a home in Baltimore, is provided by the Baltimore Symphony Orchestra. Performing its first concert in the Lyric Theatre in 1916, the BSO has come to be recognized as one of the great symphony orchestras in the world. Under the leadership of Maestro Sergiu Commissiona, this ensemble has shown flair and precision, enhanced only by the opening of its new home in the Joseph Meyerhoff Symphony Hall.

The Peabody Institute founded in 1857 is a world renowned music conservatory that has grown and changed by adapting to the needs of an ever-changing society. Since its inception, the Peabody has produced musicians of great creativity and accomplishment.

The Baltimore Ballet has become one of the most outstanding regional ballet companies in the United States. It got its start in 1961 as the Maryland Ballet and reached international recognition when two of its dancers were honored with awards in competition in Russia.

Incorporated in 1950, The Baltimore Opera Company has also undergone change and growth, with its popularity increasing over its thirty year history. As it enters a new season, the Company will again make opera accessible to the students of Maryland.

Center Stage is another example of professional theatre in Baltimore at its best. Over the years it has grown and matured as an artistic institution in the community. It is a theatre that is not afraid of experimenting, as well as providing a proving ground for new works by local authors.

With recent renovations completed, the Lyric Opera House entered a new phase in its long history. Increased seating capacity (2,500) allows more to enjoy theatrical performances that are too large in scale for the Mechanic. In addition, the Lyric allows for even grander opera performances. Since its opening in 1894, the Lyric has proven to be one of the most versatile musical facilities in Baltimore.

Art in Baltimore is alive and well, and it is being given good care and appreciation.

Baltimore Museum Of Art

THE BALTIMORE MUSEUM OF ART

Situated in elegant style among the trees of Wyman Park, The Baltimore Museum of Art rises magnificently to offer much to the discriminating visitor: Renoir, Degas, Cezanne, Monet , Picasso, and the largest collection of Matisse in the world. Thanks to the wealth and interest of the Cone sisters, Claribel and Etta, Baltimore is blessed with their once-private collection brought from a 1920's visit to Paris. One of the finer features of the Museum is the Wurtzburger Sculpture Garden. In 1982, after four years of renovations and rebuilding, a new $20 million wing was dedicated. As a result of this ambitious project, many of the Museum's older collections are once again available to the public. Among these are American paintings of the eighteenth through the twentieth century, one of the largest assemblages of drawings and prints in the United States, and a wide variety of works from Europe, Africa, the Americas, and Oceania.

WALTERS ART GALLERY

The Walters Art Gallery, originally built in 1908 to house the private collections of the Walters family, was eventually willed to the city upon the death of Henry Walters, the founder's son. Henry, like his father, had a strong penchant for collecting things: art from Byzantium and Medieval and Renaissance Europe, carvings and everyday items from Egypt and the Orient, and a fine collection of illuminated manuscripts to name a very few. The original structure is a reproduction of the Palazzo Bianco of sixteenth century Genoa and features a most impressive exterior and interior courtyard. Recent exhibitions have offered the patron a look at "Egypt's Golden Age," "The Art of Living in The New Kingdom," and "The Codex Hammer of Leonardo Da Vinci."

PEABODY CONSERVATORY OF MUSIC

Dedicated on an October day in 1866, following the most sobering days in American history — the Civil War — the Peabody Institute has served the city well, graduating its one hundreth class in 1982. "The Peabody," as most Baltimoreans know it, is a combination of various architectural influences; French and English Renaissance styles abound, and on its interior one is struck by the impressive replicas of Ghiberti's Florentine Baptistry bronze doors.

George Peabody, a successful clothing merchant and international banker, contributed $1.5 million to establish the Institute. At that time he envisioned it having four distinct entities: a Conservatory of Music (which has flourished and grown out and beyond the others), a Lecture Series, a Library, and an Art Gallery. The acoustics in the Concert Hall are among the finest to be found in the country. The Library was built in 1876 and houses an immense collection of books. Five

tiers of balconies with their ornate iron trappings containing texts, overlooks a central courtyard behind Mount Vernon Place. Original manuscripts of some of the world's finest composers, including Handell and Beethoven, can be found in the rare music collection.

At the heart of the Institute one finds the most inevitable aspect of a young concert artist's life: competition. Built into the life at Peabody is its own competitions: The Peabody Concourse (a Conservatory wide competition for any instrumentalist) and The Peabody Concerto Competition (for a specified instrument).

Since its founding in 1857, the Peabody has given the world musicians of uncommon creativity and accomplishment and given the city a showcase of which it can be most proud.

MARYLAND INSTITUTE COLLEGE OF ART
Built in the latter part of the nineteenth century in a Roman Revival style, the Maryland Institute is housed in an impressive work of art itself. This famous school of art is noted for its propensity for turning out accomplished and talented graduates (such as Edward Berge, whose work "Sea Urchin" can be found gracing the grounds of Mount Vernon Park) and for attracting inspiring artist-instructors

(like Grace Hartigan, whose works can be found in the most impressive locations about town).

Down Mount Royal Avenue, at the corner of Cathedral, the once bustling B & O Railroad Station, acquired by the Institute in 1964 as the first major public building to be recycled in the city, is now home to the Decker Gallery and Library,

studios, and the Rinehart School of Sculpture. Additional space is provided in the nearby Cannon Shoe Factory that has been turned into useable workshops, offices and a gallery.

Meyerhoff

Meyerhoff

Baltimore Ballet

Baltimore Opera

BALTIMORE BALLET

An ambitious dance company, the Baltimore Ballet was formed in 1980. Performances are presented locally and throughout the state — 130 being held in fourteen counties during the 1982-83 season. The nonprofit company has widened its scope over the past few years, and in addition to its own success has been lending space, costumes and professional advice to local dance companies.

92

BALTIMORE OPERA,

From a tragic love story like "Manon Lescaut," to Mozart's romantic comedy, "Cosi Fan Tutte," to "La Boheme" by Puccini that featured Baltimorean Pamela Myers, the Baltimore Opera Company offers a diverse schedule. Considered by many as one of the best-managed artistic endeavors in the nation, the company, with enthusiastic supporters like the late Rosa Ponselle, has given the city over thirty years of the world's best musical productions.

BALTIMORE SYMPHONY, MEYERHOFF SYMPHONY HALL

Sweeping curved walls, tons and tons of sound conditioning plaster, and suspended acoustical fiberglass clouds: the Meyerhoff Symphony Hall is itself a musical instrument. It is also a dream come true. Not only is it a dream come true for the city, but it is the culmination of the efforts of Maestro Sergiu Comissiona, Joseph Leavitt, the BSO's executive director, and Joseph Meyerhoff, whose gracious $10.5 million contribution gave birth to the dream.

Seated on the junction of Cathedral and Preston Streets, this work of art was designed by both architectural firms and acousticians. Unique among all of the concert halls of the world, the home of the Baltimore Symphony seats 2,467 in plush surroundings with an unobstructed view of the huge stage. A visual treat for the eyes and an aural treat for the ears, the Meyerhoff Symphony Hall is Baltimore's premiere showplace.

THE MECHANIC

In 1964, the same year old Ford's Theatre was sentenced to demolition, ground was broken for construction of the Morris A. Mechanic Theatre. The exposed concrete facility was designed by John M. Johansen and opened in 1967 with Betty Grable in "Hello Dolly." At the time it was the first legitimate theatre privately built in the nation in twenty five years. With the second largest subscription audience in the United States, the Mechanic is managed by the Baltimore Center for the Performing Arts — a nonprofit, tax-exempt corporation. This makes the 1600-seat theatre the only city sponsored one of its kind in the country.

Located in the heart of Charles Center, the Mechanic Theatre complex offers a multi-purpose forum for presenting largely Broadway entertainment to Baltimore area audiences. Its presentations range from hit plays and musicals to pre-Broadway try-outs, as well as special programs of dance and opera.

THE LYRIC

Built in 1894 and home for much of Baltimore's legitimate theatre performances for most of the ensuing years, the Lyric Opera House was a copy of the Leipzig Music Hall in Germany. Today, with its recent remodeling complete, the Lyric offers performances of the Baltimore Opera and contemporary theatrical shows and revivals, such as "Evita" and "Show Boat." Expanding its offerings, the Lyric is also getting into pre-Broadway shows.

CENTER STAGE

Baltimore's Center Stage, housed in a one-time wing of the old Loyola High School, has been gaining fame for the past twenty years presenting a varied menu: from Moliere to original works by Maryland authors. Its century-old quarters on North Calvert Street offers 550 seats close enough to the performance to get very involved. Theatre goers can enjoy dinner prior to a show at Oscars next door.

The Johns Hopkins University

COLLEGES & UNIVERSITIES

Baltimore has been recognized as a city concerned with higher education. In fact, education is taken quite seriously since the earliest days of the port city.

One of the earliest structures erected with the sole purpose of furthering education, is Davidge Hall on the University of Maryland Campus. In 1807 the Hall was opened as the fifth medical school in the nation, offering courses in surgery and anatomy as well as midwifery. When the public discovered that in addition to the courses mentioned, the students were utilizing corpses to practice disection, a mob ransacked the school. Today, the Hall survives as the oldest medical building in the country in continuous use.

Over the years, Baltimore schools began to spring up, attract students and gain respectable reputations. Among the most famous schools is The Johns Hopkins University. Upon the death of John Hopkins (a Quaker), $8 million was left to create a hospital and school. The Hospital, which resides on Broadway, was erected on a site selected by Hopkins himself. The University was established and Daniel Coit Gilman accepted the position of president.

Another Baltimore first was the establishment (in 1867) of a normal school to train black teachers. This school eventually became known as Bowie State College, now located in Anne Arundel County. In 1900, the local school commissioners created a school to prepare black teachers that would serve the city. This school was named for the first American black woman to earn a collegiate degree, and is known as Coppin State College.

Initially sponsored by the Methodist Conference of Baltimore, Goucher College was established and known as The Women's College of Baltimore in 1885. Throughout its significant history, Goucher has proved to be an important part of the professional and academic training for women that today is so essential.

Loyola College's role in its 132-year educational history in Baltimore is well documented. Begun in 1852 with 58 male students, the school has the best of Catholic and contemporary education. The school offers the largest M.B.A. program in the state and a new graduate degree in pastoral counseling.

The large, beautiful campus that is home to Towson State University represents considerable growth since its inception as the Maryland State Normal School in 1865. From a student body of 48 women, the University now educates nearly 14,000 men and women from all parts of the country and foreign nations.

Due to the efforts of the Methodist Conferences of Baltimore and the eventual gift of Dr. Lyttleton Morgan, the Centenary Biblical Institute was established in 1867 and went on to become Morgan State University. Among its many programs today, Morgan offers unique degrees in landscape architecture, city and regional planning, architecture, and telecommunications.

The University of Maryland got its start in Baltimore city. The campus today comprises seven schools that include law, medicine, nursing, pharmacy, dental, social work, and community planning, plus graduate studies. The University of Maryland, Baltimore County campus has become nationally recognized. With more than 7,000 students, the 17-year-old campus has been ranked in the top 5% of arts and sciences colleges in the nation.

The College of Notre Dame of Maryland was begun in 1848 as an effort of the School Sisters of Notre Dame. The North Charles Street campus that exists today is an extension of an academy they moved to in 1873.

Located at Charles Street and Mount Royal Avenue, the University of Baltimore has an enrollment of over 5,000. Its new multi-million dollar Law Center opened in 1982 and houses a 100,000 volume law library. Another of the interesting aspects of the Center is its 160-seat moot courtroom.

Another major contribution to the educational life of Baltimore has been made by the community colleges that serve the needs of area students. Dundalk Community College opened its doors in 1971, offering both day and evening programs. Unique new programs were added to the 1982 curriculum that deal with specific careers; they were Physical Fitness Technology, Data Processing, Industrial Electricity / Electronics Maintenance Technology, and Water Systems Technology.

The Community College of Baltimore is serving the city as it has since 1947 in a most pragmatic fashion, offering courses that meet specific needs in the community. A Center for English as a second language was established to serve foreign students and immigrants; the Liberty Campus Child Development Center provides programs for children in a preschool setting.

Now some twenty-six years old, Essex Community College is meeting the special needs of the varied student body it serves. Business courses are now offered in the new Business and Management Center, opened as part of the school's long-range building program. The College is now part of an even larger project; its campus cable television channel is now offered to Caltec subscribers in Baltimore County.

Catonsville Junior College in its twenty-sixth year of operation continues to be innovative. For example, the data processing curriculum has been enhanced by the acquisition of a computer terminal that talks and makes the curriculum accessible to blind and visually impaired students.

Baltimore is fortunate to have the high level of educational facilities available to its citizens that it does. The historic seeds that these schools have sown around the city and nation have had more positive effects than any of us could ever note.

JOHNS HOPKINS UNIVERSITY

A privately-endowed university, with campuses in Baltimore and Washington, D.C., Johns Hopkins was founded in 1876. It was the first American educational institution dedicated to research. As a result, it became a model for advanced study in the United States. Since its first president, Daniel Coit Gilman, took office, Johns Hopkins has been a recognized leader in American education, establishing many standards incorporated into some of the finer schools in the nation. A major attraction on the Homewood Campus is the federal style mansion (Homewood House) from which the campus derives its name. Homewood House was once the home of Charles Carroll, Jr.

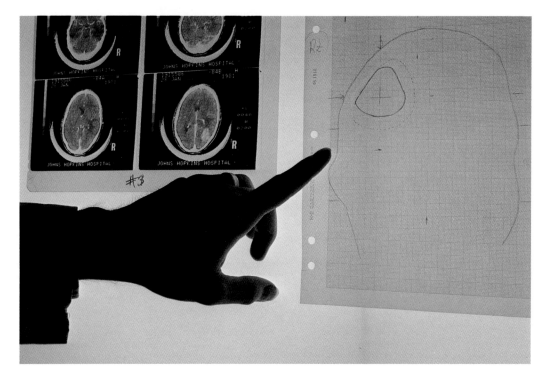

JOHNS HOPKINS HOSPITAL

Opening in 1889 on a site personally selected by its benefactor, The Johns Hopkins Hospital was followed by The Johns Hopkins University School of Medicine four years later. Together, they revolutionized the training of physicians with the introduction of clinical teaching at the patients bedside. In 1983, Hopkins scientists were the first to see the tiny structures inside the brain responsible for motion and emotion.

SHOCK TRAUMA, SHEPPARD PRATT, CHILDREN'S HOSPITAL

The shock trauma center of the Maryland Institute for Emergency Medical Service Systems (MIEMSS) is located at the University of Maryland Hospital. The brainchild of Dr. R. Adams Cowley, the shock trauma center is regarded around the world for providing the finest in emergency medical services. Working against time, the center deals directly with the critical care treatment required to face today's neglected disease — trauma.

Shock Trauma

Sheppard Pratt

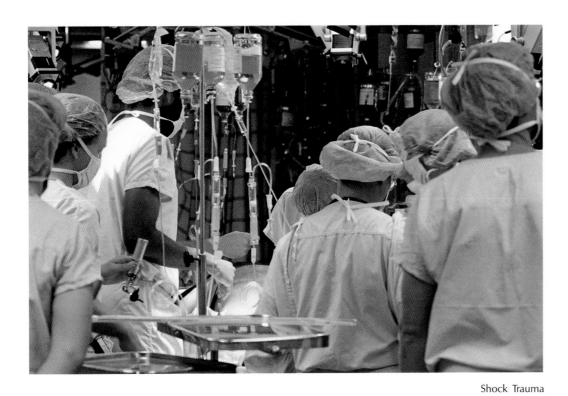

Shock Trauma

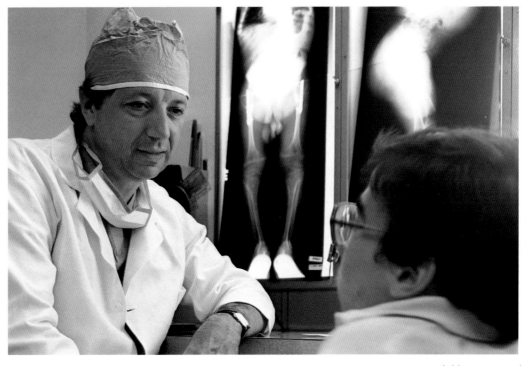

Children's Hospital

The Sheppard and Enoch Pratt Hospital is renowned for its psychiatric care. In recent years it has offered the community at large a variety of lectures and seminars, as well as personal development courses dedicated to personal growth and success. As they put it, living successfully is a learned art that can be taught, refined and perfected.

The Children's Hospital has for many years been recognized for the fine work it has done in serving Baltimore. Recently, the Hospital has been the home for Dr. Steven Kopits and his Little People's Research Fund. Dr. Kopits is considered the leading surgeon in the world today, concentrating efforts on prevention and correction of the deformities that occur especially in the hips and legs of children and adults suffering from dwarfism.

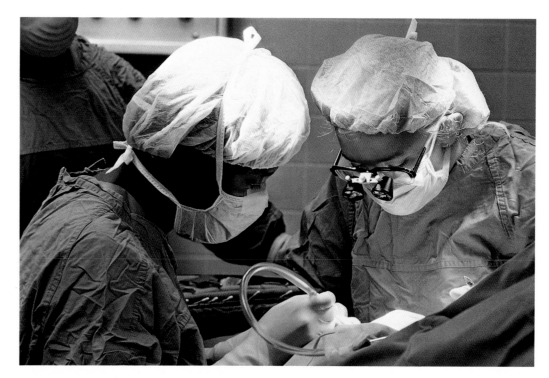

UNIVERSITY OF MARYLAND

The University of Maryland at Baltimore can be said to be the first of the state schools, and has a very vivid history. In 1807 Davidge Hall became the fifth medical school in the nation and remains the oldest medical education building in continuous use. The School of Law was founded in 1812 and was the first to provide American law students with a clearly defined educational

framework. 1840 saw the first dental school in the world established in Baltimore which later became part of the University. The School of Pharmacy (1841), the School of Nursing (1889). . . the history could fill volumes.

Today the School of Medicine sponsors a wide range of service programs, including the Down's Syndrome Center and the Sudden Infant Death Syndrome Institute. The University of Maryland at Baltimore continues to prepare and educate the health care, legal and social service professionals of tomorrow. Its medical complex provides the highest quality care for patients and a major research center which has focused in on such problems as the causes for hypertension, breast cancer, and epilepsy.

UNIVERSITY OF BALTIMORE

In the heart of Baltimore is a school which, since its inception, has offered pragmatically-oriented programs to prepare students for careers in government, business, the professional and non-profit sectors. The University of Baltimore founded in 1925 as an evening school has come a long way. In 1970 it merged with Eastern College and its Mount Vernon School of Law. Later, in 1973 it affiliated with the Baltimore College of Commerce. This school, proud of its 58-year contribution to the city and state, became a public institution in 1975.

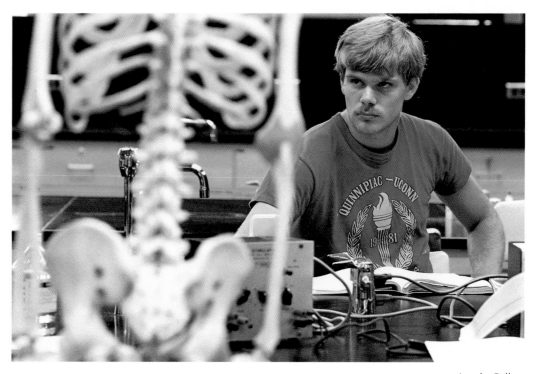

LOYOLA COLLEGE

Providing the best of Catholic and Jesuit education, Loyola College was established in 1852 by Father John Early and eight Jesuit confreres. Initially on Holliday Street, now a part of the War Memorial Plaza, the school moved in 1855 to a site on Calvert and Madison Streets (currently a portion of the original building is used as Center Stage). Referred to by most Baltimoreans as "the College," Loyola eventually moved to the present Evergreen campus in 1922. Providing some of the finest business and professional people in the city, Loyola is its own best example of the school motto: "Strong Truths — Well Lived."

MORGAN STATE

    With an eye to the future, Morgan State University, got its start in Baltimore as the Centenary Biblical Institute in 1867. It moved to its current location on Hillen Road at the end of World War I and has continued to grow considerably over the years. In 1982 one of the major events in the history of this institution occurred when the State Board of Education gave its approval to a doctoral program in Urban Educational Leadership. Over the past 116 years Morgan State has done more than graduate students; the school has given the community, the state, and the nation productive and professional graduates who have enhanced the fields they enter.

TOWSON STATE UNIVERSITY

Originally known as State Normal, with fewer than 1000 students, Towson State University obtained its current status in 1976. With a current total enrollment of over 14,000, Towson State offers over 40 undergraduate degrees and 14 programs for master's degrees. Constantly striving to stay abreast of the needs of its students, a new degree has been offered in computer science. Among its many fine programs, it is particularly proud of its fine dance and and theatre arts programs. With the completion of Towson Center, a modern spectator building, the surrounding area has available a convenient entertainment facility that has attracted the likes of Ray Charles, tennis classics, the Boston Pops, and Ronald Reagan.

Towson State University

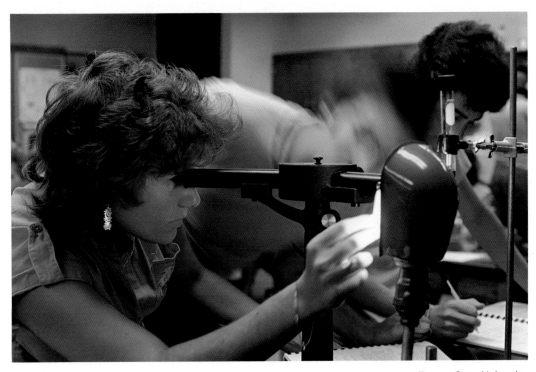

Towson State University

Goucher College

GOUCHER COLLEGE

Founded in 1885 as The Woman's College of Baltimore, Goucher took its present name in 1910 to honor its second president. In 1953, the school completed its move from cramped downtown quarters to a new campus in Towson. With more than 1,000 students from some 41 states and 20 countries,

Goucher is an independent college for women that maintains a strong liberal arts tradition, while expanding its offerings to enable women to better prepare for new career opportunities. Computer literacy in all disciplines has become a keystone of a Goucher education.

Basilica Of The Assumption

RELIGIOUS INSTITUTIONS

In the earliest illustrations of the city known as Baltimore Town one can usually find a church. Religion, of course, had played an important role in the founding of the Maryland colony, and such was the case in the creation of the town built on the Patapsco River.

From the completion of the brick structure that became St. Paul's Church in the 1730's, at what is now Charles and Saratoga Streets, to the dedication of the Cathedral of Mary Our Queen in the mid-twentieth century, Baltimore's religious institutions have played a significant role in the development of the city and its people.

Changing complexions within communities have not hindered the efforts of dedicated congregations. The devastation of fires and floods have not stopped the work of the city's religious leaders. Each new test was and continues to be met with adaptation, innovation and resolve.

As you travel the streets of the city, take note of the obvious influence these imposing structures must have had on the people in their congregation. One such leader was Father John Carroll who in 1789 became the first Roman Catholic Bishop in this country. There was Philip William Otterbein, who led the congregation at what today is the oldest standing church structure in the city, and his friend, Francis Asbury, who was the nation's first Methodist Bishop. Then there was the American-born saint, Elizabeth Ann Seton, who came to Baltimore in 1807 and opened a school for girls. She was an inspiration to the community she served, and the work she did as Mother Seton, leading the Daughters of Charity, led to her cannonization.

The German Reformed, the Scotch-Irish Presbyterians, the Jews of Europe and Russia, the Baptists and their Great Awakening revivals of the 1740's, the fleeing Acadian Catholics: all of these, plus many other important groups have made their contribution to the growth of religion in Baltimore and throughout Maryland.

MOUNT VERNON METHODIST CHURCH

Sitting across the street from a statue of Chief Justice of the Supreme Court (Roger Brooke Taney), one encounters the most elegant of Baltimore's nineteenth century churches: Mount Vernon Place United Methodist Church on Washington Place. Constructed of Baltimore County serpentine, at a cost of $325,000 in 1872, this Gothic structure was the design of Thomas Dixon and Charles Carson. It boasted the largest organ in the city and a popularity that once required an auction for choice of pews. The site upon which the church was erected was the location of the home in which Francis Scott Key died. Some 34 years before an ordinance prohibited any structure within one block of the Washington Monument that would be taller than the imposing memorial, the elaborate spires of the church rose just short of the restrictive height.

OLD ST. PAUL'S CHURCH

Old St. Paul's Church on Charles Street at Saratoga, the fourth to stand on this spot, was built on the foundations of a lavish Federal-period church that burned in 1854. The current structure is a combination of Classical architecture with the flair of Gothic. It's rectory, at Saratoga and Cathedral Streets was built in 1789 before the current church and is the oldest house in Baltimore in continuous use as a residence.

Lloyd Street Synagogue

Lloyd Street Synagogue

LLOYD STREET SYNAGOGUE

With the distinction of being the first synagogue built in Maryland and the third oldest in the United States, the Lloyd Street Synagogue today serves as a museum for the Jewish Historical Society of Maryland. Built in 1845, this was the first of four synagogues to appear in the city during the 1840's. Situated in Jonestown, the Lloyd Street Synagogue represents a historical and architectural first. Its preservation allows future generations to appreciate the religious and cultural contributions made to Baltimore by its first Jewish settlers. The Baltimore Hebrew Congregation, which was first located in the Lloyd Street Synagogue, moved over the years to its present site on Park Heights Avenue. Other congregations, like Oheb Shalom and Har Sinai, are making contributions to the communities they serve. The Beth El reform congregation was begun in 1945 now in its third generation, the synagogue is located on Park Heights Ave.

Beth El Synagogue

FIRST AND FRANKLIN STREET UNITED PRESBYTERIAN CHURCH

Built between the years 1854 and 1859, the First and Franklin Street Presbyterian Church is a masterpiece of what has been called Lancet Gothic. One of the most striking features is a triple-vaulted ceiling with massive pendants considered by many to be the most splendid victorian plaster interior in North America. Many years before the advent of the skyscraper, the church's steeple was erected with structural iron to a height of 273 feet.

Greek Orthodox Cathedral

Mary Our Queen

GREEK ORTHODOX

The Greek Orthodox Cathedral of the Annunciation, proclaimed the Cathedral of the State of Maryland by Archbishop Iakovos in 1975, stands as a testimony to the efforts of members of the parish who dedicated themselves to the growth and prosperity of their congregation over the years. Since the first Greek families began to arrive in Baltimore in large numbers in the 1880's, there has been a thirst for Orthodox worship in the community. The first place of worship was established at Bond and Gough Streets through the direct efforts of Christos Sempeles, a confectioner, and his brothers. As the congregation grew there was a need for a larger structure. The present site was selected and consecrated in 1938. Today the congregation serves as a leader in the Orthodox life of the city and state.

MARY OUR QUEEN

Ground was broken for a new Catholic Church in October 1954, but even the architect's drawings of the future structure could not match the magnificent results. The Roman Catholic Cathedral of Mary Our Queen, which was designed in contemporary Gothic styling, was made possible by an endowment from Thomas O'Neill, a Baltimore merchant. Within the sanctuary is a beautiful high altar, stained glass windows by French artist, Max Ingrand, and a classic organ with 5,600 pipes. The 270 foot long building, which has two 134 foot towers of stone that flank the main entrance, was opened in November of 1959.

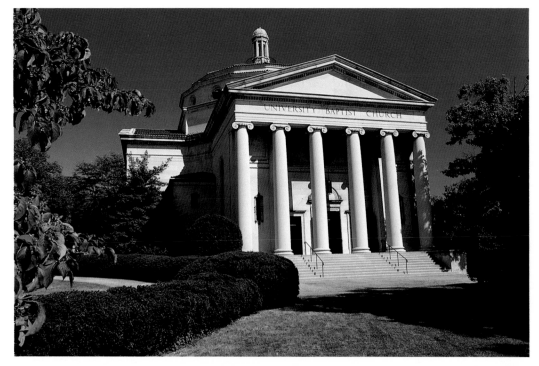

University Baptist

Old Otterbein Methodist

University Baptist

UNIVERSITY BAPTIST, OLD OTTERBEIN METHODIST

The University Baptist Church on North Charles Street was conceived in 1916 by a group of Baptist laymen who were dedicated to the establishment of a church in the rapidly developing area close to the new Homewood Campus of The Johns Hopkins University. In 1920, a chapel was dedicated, replacing the portable chapel that had been in use since 1917. The present main sanctuary was designed by the renowned John Russell Pope in a classic Italian Renaissance

style and dedicated in 1927. Over the years, the congregation has been served by an impressive list of dedicated pastoral leaders.

Old Otterbein United Methodist Church dates from 1771. Erected in 1785, the present structure is "the oldest church in town." It was erected on land purchased from John Eager Howard. Its most illustrious leader was Philip Wilhelm Otterbein, whose body is buried on the church grounds. It is interesting to note

ZION LUTHERAN CHURCH

Ripe in history and tradition, Zion Lutheran Church, known as the Lutheran Mother Church of Baltimore, was founded in 1755. Inside its historic walls are early editions of the Bible with multilingual first translations. The congregation also boasts a library of historic volumes numbering nearly 15,000, some dating back to 1539.

that the bricks used in the construction of the church were brought from England as ballast in ships and abandoned at the docks of Baltimore. The original construction costs were approximately $6,000 of which Otterbein himself donated $2,136. With the exception of the roof renewal in 1977, no major exterior changes have been made to the building in 198 years.

BASILICA OF THE ASSUMPTION

Designed in 1806 by Benjamin Latrobe, the brand-name architect of his day, the Basilica of the Assumption was officially dedicated in 1821 and became the first Catholic Cathedral in the United States. In 1979 when the United States Postal Service issued four stamps that honored American architecture; the Basilica was one of the structures illustrated. A Scandinavian visitor to Baltimore in 1818 observed the construction of the domed and columned building on Cathedral and Mulberry Streets and found its architecture "noble." Today the description fits — even after 160 some years.

ST. VINCENT DE PAUL R.C. CHURCH

St. Vincent De Paul Roman Catholic Church was established as the first parish church in Baltimore in 1840 and served the masses of immigrants coming into the port. The church is on the National Register of Historic places. In 1940 the beautiful stained glass windows were put in place and the flooring of the building is original. An interesting piece of history is the fact that at one time the church held a special 2 a.m. "printer's mass" on Sundays.

Baltimore Orioles

SPORTS

Sports and Baltimore go together as much as Crabs and Beer; and the history of sports in this community goes back a long way.

Baseball got its start in 1859 when a local shopkeeper, George Beam, got a team together and named them the Excelsiors in honor of a team by the same name in Brooklyn, New York, the name Orioles first appeared in 1883. That team was owned by brewery king, Harry von der Horst. Considering that other teams were also run by men in the same line of work, it is no wonder the league was known as "The Beer and Whiskey League."

Some think that Casey of "Casey at the Bat" was none other than Dennis Patrick Casey, an outfielder with the Baltimore Orioles in 1884-85. Jack Dunn, owner of the minor league Orioles, is supposed to have sold three players to the Boston Red Sox in 1914 for a reported $8,500. One of those players was George Herman "Babe" Ruth.

It is also worthy to note that during all of the years prior to the resurgence of major league baseball in Baltimore in 1954 there were significant contributions to baseball being made by the black ball clubs of Baltimore. The Baltimore Elite Giants, for example, won the Negro World Series in 1949 and gave the sport such players as Roy Campanella. Black baseball had gotten its start as far back as 1874 with the creation of the Lord Hamiltons and the Orientals; later there were the Lord Baltimores and the Baltimore Black Sox.

After the opening of the 1954 season Baltimore was once again back in professional baseball. With an opening day parade and 20,000 styrofoam baseballs to throw to the eager crowds, the Orioles played their first game at Memorial Stadium and beat the Chicago White Sox 3-1.

A year prior to the arrival of the Orioles, the city was selected as the home of National Football League's Colts. With its name taken from the extinct Baltimore team, the Colts started its first season with players like tackle, Art Donovan, and defensive end, Gino Marchetti. In their very first game, they stunned the Chicago Bears 13-9 and ended their first season with a 3 and 9 record.

Over the years the Colts picked up some outstanding players that eventually led to their taking the NFL Championship in 1958: Gene (Big Daddy) Lipscomb, Alan Ameche, Lenny Moore, Raymond Berry, Jim Parker, and Johnny Unitas. In 1972 the Colts won their first Super Bowl Championship by defeating the Dallas Cowboys 16-13. In that Game Johnny Unitas threw 3 passes for 88 yards and 1 touchdown and Earl Morrall threw 7 passes for 147 yards. The game was won by a Jim O'Brien field goal with nine seconds left in the fourth quarter.

With the weather in its favor, the Preakness can draw the largest sporting crowd in Baltimore. May comes alive with activities that kick off the Preakness. Thanks to the efforts of the owners of Pimlico, local businesses, television coverage, and the general interest of the public, Preakness Week has become as much of a tradition as the race itself. In 1982 a new Preakness event was initiated: the Parade of Lights. This gala dedicated to the children of Baltimore, was sponsored by WBAL Radio and featured nearly 150 floats.

The first Preakness was held in 1873 and the winner was a bay colt named "Survivor." Since that first Preakness, there have been a few changes and alterations, but these facts remain: (1) since 1931 the race has always been run on Saturdays, (2) following the results of the race, the jockey on the weathervane atop the Clubhouse is painted with the winner's racing colors, (3) the track's infield is promoted each year as the most popular location to watch the race, be entertained, and watch lacrosse games.

Baltimore and its surrounding neighbors have had a love affair with riding. Maryland Hunt Clubs, such as the Green Spring Valley Hounds and the Elkridge-Harford Hunt, have traditions going back many years. In fact, the American tradition of owning private packs of hunting hounds goes back to the days of Lord Baltimore in the 1650's. Back when Mount Vernon Place was a wooded hillside, horse and rider would gallop in pursuit of foxes.

Lacrosse, which originated as an exercise to train young warriors for combat among the Indians of North America, is among the most popular sports in Baltimore. Since the sport was first introduced to the United States in the 1870's, its popularity has grown, to what some might call a fever pitch. When the sport hit Baltimore in 1879, no one would have guessed that today the city would be the capital of lacrosse.

A highlight for all lovers of the sport was the arrival of what many called the "lacrosse olympic." In 1982 Johns Hopkins became the site of "World Lacrosse '82," which pitted teams from Canada, Australia, England and the United States. With crowds stuffed into Homewood Field, the United States went on to take the round robin event defeating the Australians 22-14 for the championship.

No final word on sports could be made about Baltimore, until something has been said about the influence the Chesapeake has had on Baltimoreans and all Marylanders. Sailing, and boating in general, has been a popular sport for generations. Besides being a provider of food and jobs for thousands of residents, the waters of Maryland have provided some of the finest recreation to be found in the nation.

Whatever the sport, be it jousting (the official State sport) or sitting on a pier and fishing, the possibilities are endless. Sports are a vital part of life in Baltimore, and Baltimore without its famous teams, like the Orioles, the Colts, the Blast, or the Skipjacks, would not be the same. Baltimore without the Preakness would not be the same. And Baltimore without sailing or lacrosse would not be the same.

MEMORIAL STADIUM — BASEBALL

Over the years, the Orioles have given the city many proud moments: its first bonus baby, pitcher Billy "Digger" O'Dell; the leadership of Paul Richards, "The Wizard of Waxahachie;" the management of Earl Weaver; Boog Powell, the team's all-time home run hitter (303) with the most grand slams (7); its first $1 million player, Eddie Murray; and who could ignore the contributions made to the sport

by Brooks Robinson. Brooks, who played longer with the Orioles than any other player, who had 16 Golden Gloves and appearances in 18 All-Star Games, who holds 9 major league records as a third baseman, who played in 4 World Series, is Mr. Oriole and to many in Baltimore, Mr. Baseball.

The Orioles have been making things happen at Memorial Stadium for nearly thirty years and the fans have been supporting the team throughout. Any day or evening at the stadium could be likened to a carnival. With hot dogs, beer, Wild Bill Hagy, peanuts, endless souvenirs, soda, the Oriole Bird, Bull Pen Parties, and those Orioles fans, there is nothing quite like a ball game at Memorial Stadium. And most importantly, there is nothing quite like those Orioles.

SKIPJACKS

Although, Baltimore has had a professional Ice Hockey team since 1963 the Skipjacks franchise has only been in Baltimore for three years. The team is locally owned thanks to the efforts of The Baltimore Hockey Advocates, a group of 25 local businessmen who own the team. Ice Hockey, originated in Canada, has developed into a very skilled and fast paced sport. The Skipjacks are working hard to increase awareness of the sport and its visibility in the city. Last year attendance rose by 33%. The Skipjacks are also working hard to give more Baltimore youth the opportunity to play Ice Hockey first hand through numerous youth leagues.

THE BLASTS

Soccer, the world's most popular sport, came to Baltimore only four years ago with the formation of the Baltimore Blasts. They are currently the champions of the major indoor soccer league. Indoor soccer differs only slightly from outdoor soccer in that the field is slightly smaller and faster because it is carpeted. Baltimore and the Blasts seem to be the perfect combination. Besides being the league champions, the Blasts also hold the league record for sellout games.

HORSE RACING

Pimlico, named for a section of London, is home to great Thoroughbred racing. "Old Hilltop" as it has long been known, has seen some fascinating Preakness events take place over the years. Aloma's Ruler, owned by Baltimorean Nathan Scherr, won well over $200,000 in 1982 as compared with the purse of $2,050 in the first running in 1873. Sixteen-year-old "Cowboy" Jack Kaenel was the youngest jockey to win the Preakness; this Baltimore County boy was riding Aloma's Ruler in 1982 and beat out veteran Willie Shoemaker. The jockey who rode in the most Preakness races was Eddie Arcaro; he rode in 15.

LACROSSE

Men's lacrosse is a contact sport. It is essentially a carrying and passing game with hard checking and blazing shots fired at the goalkeeper. There is a beauty to the proper execution of a play and an almost graceful appearance to the players captured and frozen in the midst of action. However, do not be fooled, lacrosse is a fast-paced game of skill and stamina. The play is swift and furious. And lacrosse

offers action and spontaneous excitement for both the players and the spectators.

Getting started City and Poly high schools got it introduced to the public school boys. There was hardly a local prep school that didn't pick up the sport. Since the 1920's teams like Johns Hopkins, Maryland and Navy have been dominate forces. In addition, club lacrosse has been popular among former college lacrosse stars, with the Mount Washington team standing out. Today the competition among top local players is keen for selection by the collegiate team of their choice, as young men from public and private schools in the area are scouted by the prestige teams in the country.

BOATING

From foot power to motor power to wind power, the variations are as numerous as the enthusiasts who ply the waters of the Inner Harbor and the Chesapeake Bay. The sailing craft that come into Baltimore's Inner Harbor are a sight to behold. One doesn't have to know the difference between tacking and jibing or a boom vang from battens to appreciate the grace with which the craft

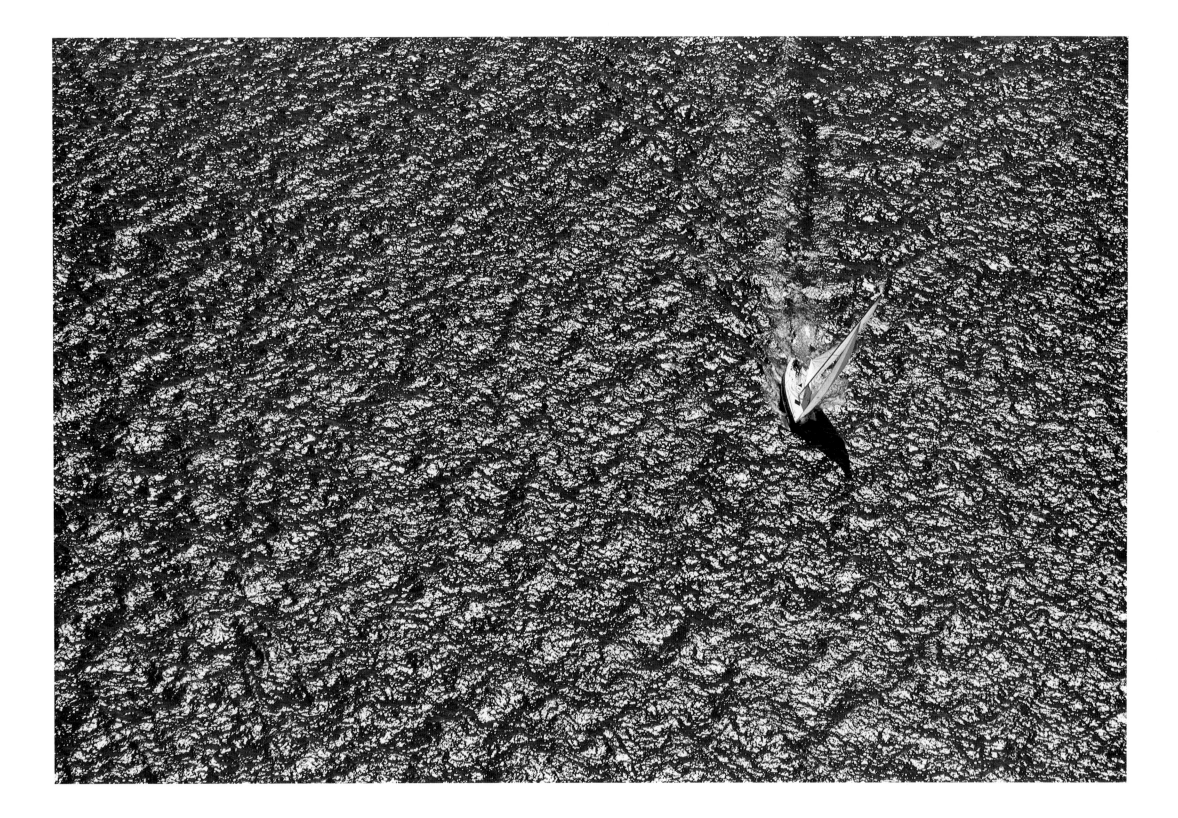

perform. One of the most popular sports in Maryland, boating provides almost as much pleasure to the nonsailor who sits on shore and enjoys the view as it does for the sailor who does all the work.

From the Inner Harbor to Kent Narrows, sailors hit the open water in every type of vessel. The marinas are booked well in advance and new sailors join the throngs by the hundreds each year. Although there is a distinct difference between the sailboats that maneuver the Chesapeake and the power craft that ply the same waters, both have made an ample contribution to the income of the area and the pleasure of millions.

NONPROFESSIONAL HORSE RACING — HUNT CUP

One of the more popular and public events for horse and rider, as well as spectator, is the Maryland Hunt Cup. Held during the steeplechase season, the Hunt Cup is considered the world's most difficult timber race. Comprised of some twenty-two jumps (the jumps being constructed of logs) the course is four miles in length around a circuit of fields, considered by many to be quite dangerous. Competition is the name of the game, and some of the jumps have taken their toll. One jump, for example, has been nicknamed the Union Memorial. It is this five foot jump, over five logs, that has killed horses and injured riders.

With horse and rider seemingly one with another, competition is beautiful as well as keen at the Maryland Hunt Cup. Each year thousands of horse lovers and the curious gather on beautifully wooded pastures with names like Snow Hill and Worthington Farms to watch the flashes of color in this prestigious, yet very dangerous event. For many it is being near such a competitive event with all of its tension and grace that is most important; for others it is being a part of the buzz of socializing. Whatever the reason, the Hunt Cup is one of Maryland's true sporting events.

CITY SERVICES

The Baltimore city government is one of the most responsive and responsible of any major city in the nation. The city is an independent political jurisdiction within the state of Maryland. Baltimore city delivers services to the various levels of its population much too extensive to elaborate fully in this book. Some of the major services which are provided are outstanding police and fire departments, a public school system, water and sewage, garbage removal, maintenance of city roads and facilities, as well as the coordination of the various economic and logistical needs of its population.

Baltimore city is successful because it is not only responsive but it also has developed strong financial management which has been able to successfully implement its plans. The city has a 1980 "A" rating from Standard and Poor's and a A-1 from Moody's. Sound management combined with creative imagination has successfully allowed the city to develop such innovative programs as the dollar house program. This project took abandoned houses in the city and for one dollar and a commitment to restore the structure within two years made these houses available to willing participants. So successful was this program that lotteries had to be held to determine who would get what house. Needless to say this program also redeveloped neighborhoods which were badly in need of attention.

Baltimore city has also been a successful catalyst in developing plans which are participated in by various private organizations as well as the state and federal governments. The prime example of this is the development of the Charles Center project with the redevelopment of the downtown area.

Baltimore city has developed various "satellite" support organizations to facilitate the development of the city. These organizations work with and for the city government but are not directly administered or financed in total by the city. Some of these are the GBC (Greater Baltimore Committee), The Charles Center, Inner Harbor Management Committee, The Promotion and Tourism Council, The Baltimore Briefing Center as well as The Baltimore Convention Bureau.

Creative, diversified, sound management policies have been responsible for the development of unparalleled success for the city of Baltimore.

FIRE DEPARTMENT

Today's modern Baltimore City Fire Department with some 2,195 positions and a budget that exceeds $63 million, is broken down into eight bureaus or divisions and has the direct responsibility of protecting the city and its citizens from fire and providing ambulance service. Along with 58 fire stations strategically located around Baltimore, the Fire Department maintains a Repair Shop, Headquarters, and Fire Academy. There are also 52 engine companies, 29 truck companies, 1 rescue company, 16 ambulances, and 2 fire boats. High technology and the use of computerized equipment are employed to speed information when help is needed. In addition, advanced training programs insure that Baltimore has some of the best firemen in the nation.

POLICE

The Baltimore Police Department has a rich heritage that goes back to the 1790's. Today's city police are well equipped and well trained to service the needs of the population it serves. Currently one of the strongest efforts ever is being directed at crippling drug sales and distribution in Baltimore. The helicopter unit celebrated ten years of service in 1981 with impressive statistics: over 100,000 calls for service, contributing to over 4,400 arrests. In its attempt to stay current and meet the special needs of citizens, a Deaf Awareness training course has been offered to the force.

ENOCH PRATT LIBRARY

Opened to the public on January 4, 1886, the Enoch Pratt Library then held some 20,000 volumes in the main building and approximately 3,000 volumes in each of four branches. Today the Pratt system comprises some 34 locations around the city and is a veritable gold mine of materials for children, adults, teachers, senior citizens, and the researcher. In addition to the obvious books, the library provides movies, puppet shows, story hours, reading classes, and summer reading programs. The yearly budget is nearly $5 million.

METRO CENTER

The downtown central city core is today a gleaming example of the "new" Baltimore. It is a credit to the years of work and imagination of numerous dedicated city administrators and planners. From a central city that was experiencing decay and neglect and watching major businesses move to the suburbs, Baltimore has created a city more alive than it ever imagined. Not only has the city generated leisure time activity that never existed in the past but it has also greatly increased business and financial activity. Office buildings are now being built and filled faster than was ever envisioned in the past.

The Charles Center project anchored the master plan for the downtown area in the 1970's. This was a successful, coordinated effort by both the public and private sector of Baltimore in the development of office, retail and residential facilities. Recreational facilities and open spaces were also a major aspect of the plan from the beginning. Two of the more popular recreational spaces are Hopkins Plaza and Charles Center Plaza.

In the expansion of the Charles Center development plan the Inner Harbor area was developed. Again this plan included a combination of commercial, retail, resident, and recreational facilities. Some of the more noteworthy developments are The National Aquarium in Baltimore, The Maryland Science Center, The World Trade Center, and Harborplace (a recreational retail complex of over 120 shops and restaurants).

Baltimore's downtown area is now the hub of a major market in its own right. With a population of 2.2 million people it buys, sells and manufactures a wide range of products and services. The median age is 29.8 years and the combined buying income is $12.7 billion. The Baltimore market supports a labor force of over one million people. This combined with the Washington, DC, market, only 40 miles to the south, creates the fourth largest market area in the country (known as "The Common Market"). The combined population is over five million people who spend more than $38.5 billion.

Baltimore's downtown metropolitan area is now a base from which the future and the growth of Baltimore and the region can and will develop beyond all expectation.

Charles Center South

Garmatz Federal Courthouse

C & P Telephone

Inner Harbor Center

RTKL ASSOCIATES INC.

A part of Baltimore for nearly four decades, RTKL Associates Inc., is one of the city's major Architectural/Planning/Engineering firms. A revitalization has spread throughout the city, so too have RTKL's design projects. Notably, Charles Center South, designed by RTKL, was responsible for a cascade of urban renewal efforts. Other projects in downtown Baltimore include the C & P Telephone

Charles Center South

Company Building; The Garmatz Federal Courthouse Building; The Metro Center at Charles and Baltimore Streets; and the Hyatt Regency Hotel. Important projects outside the downtown area are The Greater Baltimore Medical Center; additions to and renovations of the Johns Hopkins Hospital; The University of Maryland's Shock-Trauma Center Plan; The University of Maryland's Baltimore Campus in Catonsville; The New Goucher Campus Center; and the USF&G Computer Center and Training Facility in Mt. Washington. Over 300 people working in RTKL's Inner Harbor Center Building have made a major contribution to the overall revitalization of Baltimore.

Hopkins Plaza

C & P Telephone

Equitable Bank Center II

USF & G, McKeldin Plaza

Open and recreational spaces make downtown Baltimore both attractive and functional. They effectively eliminate a feeling of being closed in and overwhelmed by crowds of people. They facilitate the flow of business, retail and residential population. They also allow the use of the downtown area as a recreational complex as well as a business center.

THE PORT

The Port of Baltimore is the second largest containerport on the East Coast; that fact has not always been so. In the early days, other ports, like Annapolis and Oxford, were more successful. However, by 1706, the foundations of the port of Baltimore were firmly established and this pre-dated the incorporation of the city by more than twenty years.

With its inland location, sheltered from the open waters of the Chesapeake Bay, today's port, as in days past, has distinct commercial advantages. Today's port offers its users virtually every conceivable type of installation and service required for the swift and efficient movement of cargoes to and from any location

Diversity has always played a strong role in the importance of Baltimore as a port. During the blockade of colonial ports by King George III's naval fleet, the city was able to open new markets in the West Indies and Latin America largely due to Baltimore's ability to export tobacco. Although there was some disruption of services during the War of 1812, and specifically during the attacks on the city and Fort McHenry, the port bounced back rapidly. With the introduction of steam power to vessels, Baltimore's business expanded. With faster means of transportation, the city's potential markets grew considerably beyond the Mississippi River.

With the discovery of vast deposits of guano on islands off the coast of Peru, Baltimore shipowners took advantage of their find and introduced the city into the fertilizer and chemical industries. Along with guano, copper refining pushed Baltimore in the forefront of ports around the nation. All was going well, until the outbreak of hostilities that became the Civil War.

Trade with the south ended and trade with the western portions of the country came to a halt. Baltimore became an arsenal and naval base. However, when the war ended Baltimore regained its prominence as a major world port.

With railroad expansion and the creation of major ocean terminals along the harbor's edge, Baltimore was ready for the twentieth century. Only a disaster like the Great Fire of 1904 could set back the progress that the port had regained. Nearly $50 million worth of the Inner Harbor and the financial district was destroyed in a matter of hours. Quick to bounce back from hard times, Baltimore promptly rebuilt.

The opening of the Panama Canal followed by the first major European war in 1914 stimulated the construction of warehouses, railroad truck lines and new piers to meet the growing demand for American goods and products. During World War II, the port also became a major source of war vessels, such as the nearly 400 Liberty ships produced by the Bethlehem-Fairfield shipyards.

However, by the war's end, with railroad ocean terminals in desperate need of repair, the port fell upon very hard times. The Maryland Port Authority, which later became the Maryland Port Administration, was created in 1956 by the General Assembly. As a result of planning and concerted effort on the part of the city, the state and private businesses, the port continues to dedicate itself to the city and the excellence that Baltimore has always held in the maritime eyes of the world.

According to recent figures, the port of Baltimore is worth approximately $1.2 billion in revenues and employment to Maryland. In addition, some $52 million in state and local taxes are generated by port activity. One study shows that 79,000 Marylanders, or 4 percent of the state's total work force, have been employed by organizations related to the port.

The port represents Maryland's largest industry and possibly its most valuable resource. It has been suggested that by the late 1980's export coal through the port will reach an estimated 40 million tons a year. Export facilities now under construction will boost Baltimore's coal tonnage by 122 percent. In 1981 piers in the port moved 12.9 million tons of coal; currently its handling capacity is 18 million tons.

As in the past, speed and efficiency play a big part in keeping the customer happy. Recently 91 transit buses worth nearly $13 million were loaded on a vessel bound for Puerto Rico in just five hours. Once underway, the shipment reached its destination a mere 68 hours later.

In another dramatic example of the volume of shipping handled out of the port, one of the nation's oldest surviving lumber companies, J. Gibson McIlvain of White Marsh, ships nearly 2.4 million board feet of lumber annually through the Baltimore facilities. Owners believe that foreign trade in lumber, which now represents 12 percent of the firm's total business, is expected to increase nearly 100 percent within two years.

With marine terminals located all along the nearly 45-mile long developed shore line, Baltimore can satisfy a multitude of service needs. Currently ten full-service terminals cover the water from the Inner Harbor and Northwest Branch, to the Middle Branch, Lower Patapsco River, and Curtis Bay.

Headquartered in the modern office complex at the World Trade Center on the Inner Harbor, the Maryland Port Administration works to further the interests of the state by encouraging and facilitating international commerce. As a charter member of the World Trade Centers Association, the primary function of the Center is to expand international business by fostering the concept of World Trade Centers.

There is little doubt that the port will continue to serve the needs of commerce through continually updated facilities. Baltimore will continue to expand its scope in the area of marine services to the nation and the world.

150

TUG BOATS, CURTIS BAY, SERVICES

Founded in 1910, Curtis Bay Towing Company operates fleets in three cities, including Baltimore. It specializes in barge transportation and ship docking activity. Service is the byword of the tugs that serve the harbor of this city. The ships that come to Baltimore's harbor require twenty-four-hour-a-day attention; the tug is often its only link with shore. Many times each year tugboats are put to sea, under the most severe of weather conditions to tow disabled ships back to safety. Ore ships, coal barges, heavily laden tankers — whatever the requirement, the tugs of Baltimore harbor can fill the bill.

MARYLAND PORT ADMINISTRATION

The Maryland General Assembly created the Maryland Port Authority in 1956, to coordinate, control and plan future expansions of the port facilities. It became the Maryland Port Administration in 1971. Through its skillful management and planning, the Port of Baltimore has grown and successfully kept pace with the demands of increased international trade in the 1970's and the beginning of the 1980's.

The development of the Dundalk Marine Terminal is an example of the Maryland Port Administration's achievement to date. Purchased from the city in 1959 for $4 million the previously abandoned airport has become the center of cargo activity in the port (both container and break bulk). The complete development of Dundalk Marine Terminal has taken over twenty years and has cost more than $200 million.

DUNDALK MARINE TERMINAL

With the completion of Berth 13 in October, 1982, Dundalk's docks are now fully developed and operational. Berth 13 or "Superberth" as it is called is the largest facility in the terminal. It was constructed at a cost of $35 million and has a bulkhead of 1,050 feet in length. It is expected to add at least 750,000 tons to the port's annual cargo handling capacity.

Two 40 ton capacity container cranes, capable of handling 20 foot and

40 foot containers as well as non-containerized heavy machinery, service Berth 13. Each crane has a duty cycle of 48 movers (24 units on and 24 units off) in one hour of operation. The addition of these two cranes brings the terminal's cranes capacity to ten.

Dundalk Marine Terminal is the center of the port's cargo handling operations. But the combined port facilities now has 64 general cargo berths and 18 public bulk cargo berths. Support facilities include 25 public warehouses with over 6 million square feet of enclosed storage space and nearly 5 million cubic feet of cold storage. The future for both public and private facilities is set upon continued diversity and expansion to meet the port's needs into the 80's and 90's.

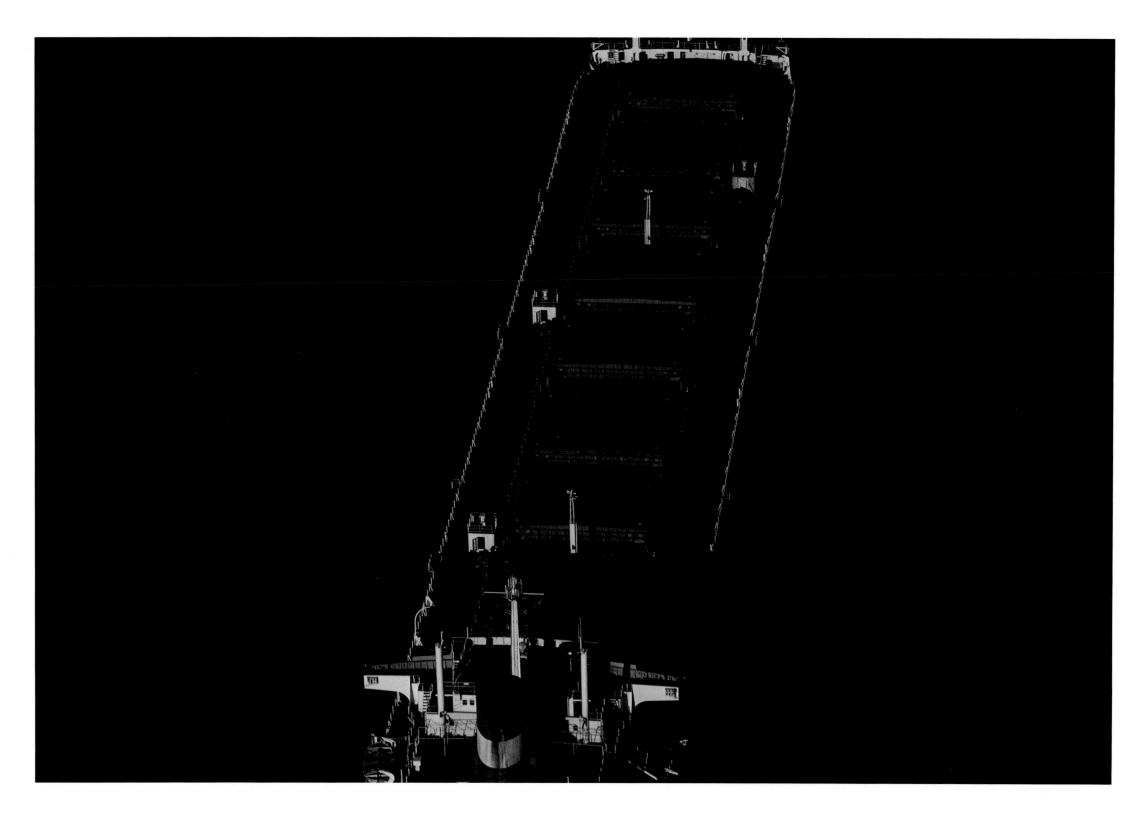

RAILROADS

Before the establishment of the Maryland Port Administration, the Port of Baltimore was previously railroad oriented. The Baltimore & Ohio Railroad, the oldest railroad in the country and the Pennsylvania Railroad built and owned virtually all the port facilities.

Today primarily rail oriented facilities are available for unloading of ore

and the loading of coal at a rate of 6,000 and 11,000 tons per hour respectively. Three grain elevators with a combined storage capacity of eleven million bushels can be loaded at a rate of 270,000 bushels per hour.

Two major trunk line rail companies service the Port of Baltimore. The CSX Corporation (Chessie System, Inc. / Seaboard Coast Line Industries, Inc.) and the Consolidated Rail Corporation (Conrail) provide the port with a vast network of rail service. Combined, this network gives the port first-day, fast freight rail delivery service to 43.7% of the United States industrial market and 36.6% of the United States population.

Francis Scott Key Bridge

TRANSPORTATION

Baltimore affords visitors and residents alike easy access to both the downtown metropolitan area and any of its outlying neighborhoods. Like most cities its size Baltimore has developed major transportation facilities to handle the needs of both population movement and business oriented transportation needs. Being one of the world's great ports these demands are awesome. Through astute planning by local, state and federal transportation agencies Baltimore has developed a very efficient mix of highways, railroads, air and local surface transportation.

Interstate highways link the center of Baltimore city to the state and every major American city. Major interstate highways which are a part of Baltimore's intricate system include 70, 83, and 95. In all Baltimore and the state of Maryland are served by 5,200 miles of highway. The Beltway (I-695) completely surrounds the city and allows easy access from one section of Baltimore to another. Both 95 and the Baltimore-Washington Parkway connect Baltimore to Washington, DC and points south. In all more than 1,000 miles of highway have been built in the last 25 years and 2/3 of the existing system has been improved.

Local streets are wide, clearly marked and layed out in a efficient square-grid pattern. This allows quick access to and from anywhere in the city. Traffic lights are also sequenced to allow a flow of traffic through and around the city.

Baltimore is served by two major railroad systems. The Conrail / Amtrack system provides north and south rail transportation for both passenger and freight. The Chessie System (a combination of the Baltimore & Ohio, Chesapeake & Ohio, Western Maryland Railways and the Seaboard Coast Line) provides Baltimore primarily with freight service north, south, and west in one of the largest rail systems in the country. Baltimore is also served by two switching lines the Canton Railroad and the Patapsco and Back River Railroad Company.

Over 100 inbound and outbound trains include the ultra-modern metroliner, provide convenient rail service to Baltimore.

The Historic Pennsylvania Station used for most passenger rail service has just undergone a major renovation. It provides both efficient and an aesthetically pleasant atmosphere for passengers using rail transportation in Baltimore.

Baltimore Washington International Airport offers Baltimore easy, quick access to one of the newest and most efficient international airports in the world. Actually BWI is not new, but has just undergone a $67,500,000 improvement project. It is located only 9 miles from the center of the city. It can be reached quickly by either taxi, airport limousine, bus or auto transportation. BWI Is capable of handling the largest aircraft flying today and is designed as one alternative field for the SST.

The Mass Transit Administration handles public transportation systems for the Baltimore metropolitan area. This includes one of the largest bus systems in the country with over 900 buses. It is also just about to finish work on phase one of the Metro (Baltimore's Rapid Rail System). Construction of the Metro began in 1976 and phase one is stated to open in November of 1983. The $797 million project is a major step in giving Baltimore one of the most efficient system of public transportation in the country. The Metro will eventually be extended east, south and west. It will be linked with bus and other public transportation facilities to give Baltimore a modern regional rapid transportation system.

Baltimore has a truly modern system of local, regional, national and international transportation. It gives residents and visitors easy access to almost anywhere in the city and the world.

BWI

Twenty-five passenger airlines serve BWI, providing nonstop service to more than 50 cities in the United States. Some 300 direct flights depart daily to both domestic and international destinations. In addition, BWI handles some 60% of the Baltimore / Washington region's total air freight volume.

Some have remarked that the new terminal at BWI seems to be airborne itself. The 1,200 foot long space frame roof, the largest of its kind in the country, is supported by ten distinctive glazed-red tile towers. The architectural concept for the structure's exterior revolves around glass and steel admitting vast amounts of light to the interior and producing an airy and spacious appearance.

Interstate 95

Pennsylvania Station

MTA Buses

Metro

METRO

The newest addition to the Baltimore transportation system is the Metro. This major project, undertaken by both federal and state transportation agencies, will be a major step in developing rapid access to the center of the city. It will when finished effectively eliminate a tremendous flow of commuter auto traffic into the city each day. Combined with park and ride bus links this will be a major development for Baltimore transportation system.

Bethlehem Steel

MANUFACTURING

Historically, Baltimore has been a good place to locate a manufacturing concern. With its port and railroads, the city was a popular location in the nineteenth century. The twentieth century has seen a lot of changes in the manufacturing trends that have affected most major cities in the East. Baltimore, with its famous port and transportation facilities and a government concerned with growth and revitalization, should continue to move ahead in attracting new industry, while retaining the base already established.

One need only look at a list of manufacturing concerns that have operations in Baltimore to understand the impact they have had on the development of the city: General Motors Assembly Division, Bethlehem Steel Corporation, Black and Decker, Koppers Company, Inc., Tate Industries, Armco Steel Company, Ellicott Machine, Noxell, and the list goes on.

In addition to the efforts of the city, major industrial employers in Baltimore have invested in massive projects to modernize existing facilities. In 1982 General Motors announced plans for a $200 million modernization and enlargement project that includes new, high technology machinery and robots. Armco Steel Company is modernizing its stainless steel plant with the installation of a continuous caster and automatic forging machine at a cost of nearly $30 million. Lever Brothers, found in the Canton section of the city, is undergoing an expansion project that will allow the local plant to produce sulphanamilid which has had to be imported in the past. The project will cost approximately $10 million.

Baltimore is not dominated by any single industry. It is a city of diverse manufacturing and industrial concerns, and some of those are continuously growing and expanding. With the likes of AAI in Cockeysville, Westinghouse and Martin-Marietta, Baltimore offers a wide range of employment opportunities.

Finally, the future of manufacturing in Baltimore looks brighter than in many other cities around the country. With the city's concern for retaining existing industry and attracting new business, Baltimore is an ideal location. Significant additions have been developed in the last few years for existing plants. One of the reasons for the success of many of these projects is the Baltimore Economic Development Corporation (BEDCO).

Ellicott Machine

Koppers

General Motors

GM, ELLICOTT MACHINE, KOPPERS

Ground was broken back in 1934 for a new Chevrolet and Fisher Body Assembly Plant for Baltimore. It was planned that the plant would produce approximately 80,000 cars and trucks each year. During World War II the plant underwent conversion to production of wartime parts and the assembling of fuselages for aircraft carrier based planes. By 1978, the plant, having undergone numerous changes during the years, produced its eight-millionth automobile.

Employing as many as 7,000 people, the facility has continued to work in the area of cars and light trucks. The success of truck assembly in Baltimore has led to a major expansion of the plant.

A leading name in dredging equipment and innovation in that industry is the Ellicott Machine Corporation of Baltimore. Founded in 1885, success was neither over night nor easy. There were many years of hard work to make

Ellicott Machine

the company and its products popular around the world. From the construction of a huge dredge commissioned by the U.S. Army Corps of Engineers for a project in California in the early part of the century to World War II transport engines, Ellicott Machine dredges are in use in more than sixty nations.

Koppers, a Fortune 500 company is a diversified manufacturing concern with multiple locations in the Baltimore area. Its Engineered Metal Products Group manufactures such products as power transmission products, sophisticated systems for controlling sound and handling solid waste, and piston rings and seals. The company had its beginnings in a firm that started in the 1830's, Bartlett-Hayward — the company that introduced the Baltimore Heater.

BETHLEHEM STEEL CORPORATION

Located at Sparrows Point, Bethlehem Steel's tidewater site was first selected in the late 1800's. After its acquisition in 1916, the facilities were greatly enlarged and today, Sparrows Point is one of the largest steel plants in the United States. Furnaces at the "Point" can annually produce about seven million tons of raw steel. With environmental quality control a concern of every modern industry, Bethlehem Steel is doing its part to ensure the natural integrity of the area.

Humphreys Creek Waste Water Treatment Plant, was constructed solely to reduce waste pollution, and high-energy wet scrubbers, working in conjunction with stacks, remove approximately 99% of all particles from gases created by the furnaces.

Often considered to be a city within a city, Sparrows Point offers a vast array of services. It also produces part of its own power needs at the Pennwood Power Station. A first-rate transportation system insures that raw materials arrive promptly at the plant and the finished product is shipped out just as quickly. During the 1970's a new pier was built to accommodate larger ore ships with drafts up to 50 feet.

Noxell

NOXELL, ALLEGHENY PEPSI

Now in its 66th year of business, Noxell continues to grow and expand its horizons giving Baltimore every reason to be proud that it had its birth here in 1914. From the pharmacy of Dr. Bunting on North Avenue to the expansive headquarters in Baltimore County, it has been a long and successful history. The new Office and Laboratory Building links the Research, Manufacturing and Administrative wings under one roof and creates a well-integrated complex that allows Noxell to take advantage of one of its strengths: teamwork.

Conducting business in some 27 states, the Allegheny Beverage Corporation is a Baltimore success story. With its acquisition of The Macke Company, in 1981, whose food service, vending and diverse operations are known to some of the largest corporations in the country, Allegheny has continued to show growth and innovation.

Carling

Allegheny Pepsi

Carling

CARLING NATIONAL BREWERIES, INC.

Built in 1960 and opened in 1961, the Carling National Brewery in Baltimore County is a subsidiary of the G. Heileman Brewing Company, Inc., which acquired Carling National in March of 1979. Earlier in 1975, Carling had merged with the National Brewing Company. In 1983 the capacity of the plant will reach a new high of 2,000,000 barrels. Its largest, and most localized beverage is National Premium Beer. In addition to local favorites, National Premium and National Bohemian, the plant also produces Colt 45 Malt Liquor, Tuborg Beer, Black Label and Wiedemann Beer.

McCormick Foods

Black & Decker

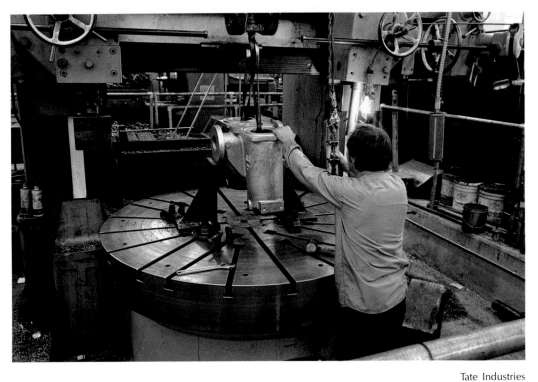

Tate Industries

Black & Decker

McCORMICK & COMPANY

McCormick & Company is a diversified specialty food company and a world-wide leader in the manufacturing and marketing of seasoning and flavoring products. The company was founded in Baltimore in 1889 and had net sales in 1982 of over $700 million.

BLACK AND DECKER, TATE INDUSTRIES

When people think of power drills, they think of Black and Decker. Since the invention of the pistol grip and trigger switch in 1916, which led to the modern power drill, Black and Decker has been involved in the development of outstanding new products, such as the Apollo Lunar Surface Drill. Black and Decker is the world's leading manufacturer and marketer of power tools. Since its beginnings in 1910, innovation has been the key to the company's

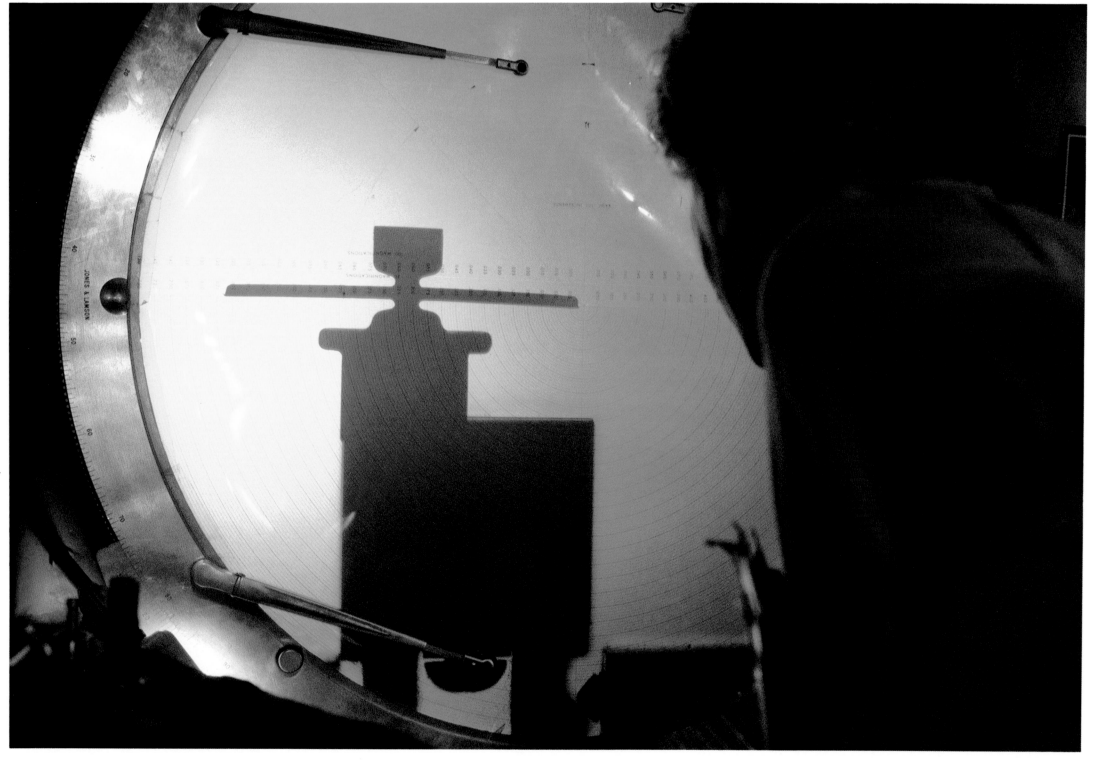

success. In addition, the Towson-based company has been driven by a desire to create labor-saving products that are affordable to the consumer.

Founded in 1924 by William J. Tate, a manufacturer's representative of replacement boiler parts for merchant ships in the port of Baltimore, Tate Industries has been transformed into a distributor of engineered products and services for industry. In addition, the company began manufacturing specialty valves, pipe line strainers and air dryers for use in industry and ship construction throughout the United States and foreign markets. Access flooring became the third leg of Tate Industries in 1964, providing entry into the growth markets of computers and office work spaces.

Londontown Manufacturing

Kirk-Stieff

Londontown Manufacturing

Kirk-Stieff

LONDONTOWN

Ranked as the world's leading producer of high quality men's and women's rainwear and outerwear, Londontown Corporation got its start in the 1930's making men's tailored clothes. A major event in the history of the company came in 1954 when, after making rainwear for the armed forces in World War II, Londontown achieved a breakthrough by creating a durable water-repellent item of rainwear that was also lightweight and breathable. It was called London Fog. Although the company was not sure if the name would catch on, today the brand name is known the world over.

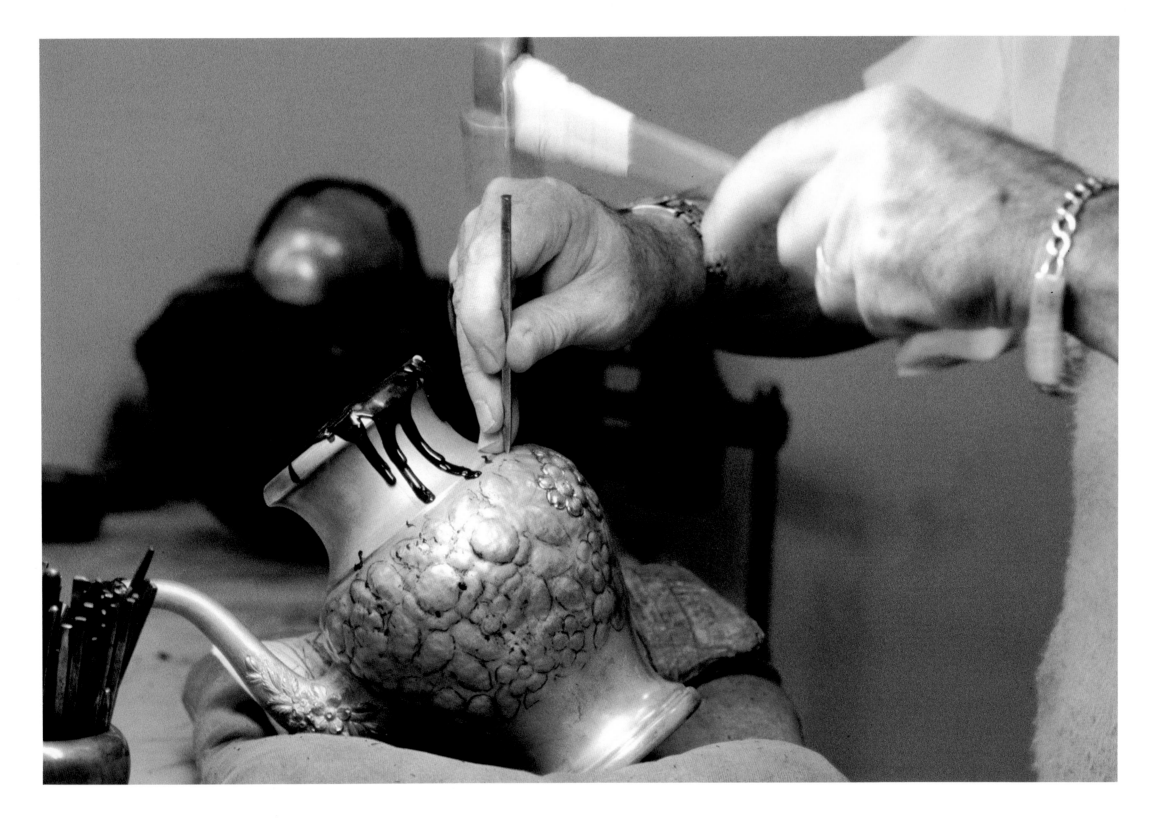

KIRK-STIEFF

With a history that goes back to 1815, the Kirk-Stieff Company gets it name from two famous Baltimore Companies that joined forces in 1979. It was Samuel Kirk who introduced the famous Repousse style of ornamentation on sterling silver, known as "Baltimore Silver." Kirk products were desired and used by the Roosevelts, Robert E. Lee and General Lafayette. The Stieff Company was founded in 1892 and was recognized for its fine sterling silverware and pewter.

From its first small shop in the Redwood Street area, the company supplied high quality flatware and holloware. In the 1930's Stieff met a national demand by supplying to fine retail jewelers and department stores. A milestone in the company's history was their selection by Colonial Williamsburg to make authentic reproductions in pewter and sterling. Today the tradition is carried on by the Stieff family.

CROWN CENTRAL PETROLEUM
    With corporate headquarters located in Baltimore, Crown Central Petroleum Corporation is a major distributor of petroleum products in Maryland and the surrounding region. Besides numerous clean, efficient retail outlets throughout the area they also have a major terminal and storage facility in Baltimore. With gross sales in excess of one billion dollars, Crown Central Petroleum Corporation is one of the 100 largest corporations headquartered in Baltimore.

BALTIMORE GAS & ELECTRIC COMPANY

The majority of the Baltimore metropolitan region energy, both natural gas and electricity, is supplied by the Baltimore Gas & Electric Company. One of the most efficient and responsive public utility companies in the nation, BG & E has held down consumer energy costs for services supplied by its system's generating capacity of 5,000,000 kilowatts. Natural gas is supplied to the area through a pipeline connector system which is supplemented by its own synthetic gas generating plant.

BG & E — CALVERT CLIFFS

Calvert Cliffs is Maryland's first commercial nuclear power plant. It is located in Calvert County on the western shore of the Chesapeake Bay. Its two nuclear generating units have supplied more than 50% of BG & E's total service requirements since 1977 when both units went into operation. The Calvert Cliff plant cost a total of $778 million to build and make operational. Its efficiency has been a major reason why the cost of electrical energy has risen less than the overall cost of living since it was put into operation. It has saved BG & E customers more than $2.8 billion in fuel costs since it became operational.

Calvert Cliffs

C & P

C & P

C & P

THE CHESAPEAKE AND POTOMAC TELEPHONE COMPANY

The Baltimore metropolitan area is supplied with telephone service by the C and P Telephone Co. of Maryland. The company directly services more than 3.5 million telephones throughout the region with some of the most advanced call-handling systems available. Advanced communication systems give it a high level of reliability in transmitting the large volume of necessary communications to the Baltimore area, the nation and the world.

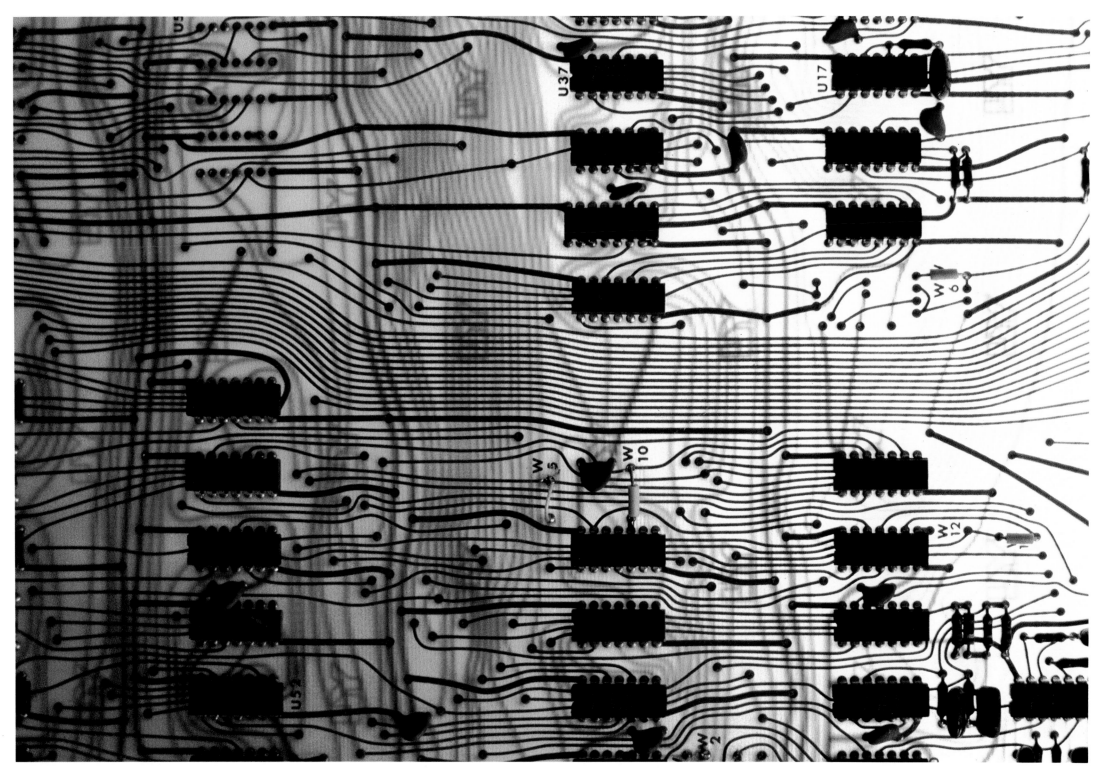

Penta Systems

HIGH TECHNOLOGY

The field of high technology is a relatively new industry which has had, from the very beginning, a large position in the commerce of Baltimore. With such major companies as Western Electric, Westinghouse and Martin Marietta having major facilities in the area, Baltimore has seen much activity in the areas of research and production of high-technology products. Growth in the field of high technology has been rapid in Baltimore over the last couple of years, both for defense and consumer products.

One factor influencing this growth is Baltimore's geographic location. Situated in the northeast with a network of easy transportation facilities for manufacturers to use, is an asset. Also, its proximity to Washington, DC and major defense and government contractors has been a major factor in this growth.

The Baltimore area also offers a large skilled and semi-skilled labor force for companies moving into the area to quickly and easily staff positions. Cost of labor in the area is moderate and the cost of land and services in the region is also very favorable.

Baltimore offers an existing pool of very skilled research and development personnel. There is over $265 million worth of research and development already going on in the Baltimore area each year. Institutions such as Hopkins and the University of Maryland have a major role in working with government and private companies with research and development projects. They are also a major source of personnel.

To date, Baltimore has a very large position in the field of high technology industries. Unparalleled growth has been seen in this field because of various factors, specifically; location, favorable costs, and a readily available skilled and semi-skilled labor force.

Penta Systems

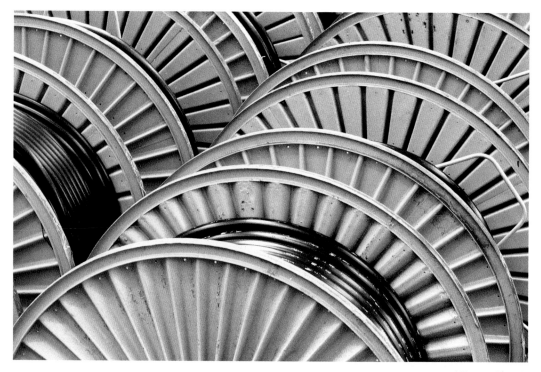

Western Electric

Western Electric

PENTA SYSTEMS INTERNATIONAL, INC.

Originally established in 1966 as a typesetting company, Penta is now a major supplier of computer automated composition systems which produce high quality typography. Today the company both assembles, installs and is a major supplier of its systems and software to clients throughout the United States and the world. Penta is an outstanding example of a growth oriented company in the field of high technology.

WESTERN ELECTRIC

Western Electric is a manufacturer and supplier of communication equipment to AT & T and other telephone companies throughout the United States and the world. With over 6,000 people employed in the area by Western Electric, it is a major part of Baltimore's high technology industry.

WESTINGHOUSE

Westinghouse is a broad based multi-national company with manufacturing, research and production facilities in the area. Numerous products related to avionics, and advanced radar systems are manufactured in these facilities. Westinghouse is also the owner and operator of WJZ-TV as well as other cable and communication facilities in the area through its broadcasting division. Employing more than 14,000 people in the region, Westinghouse is a major factor in Baltimore's high technology industry.

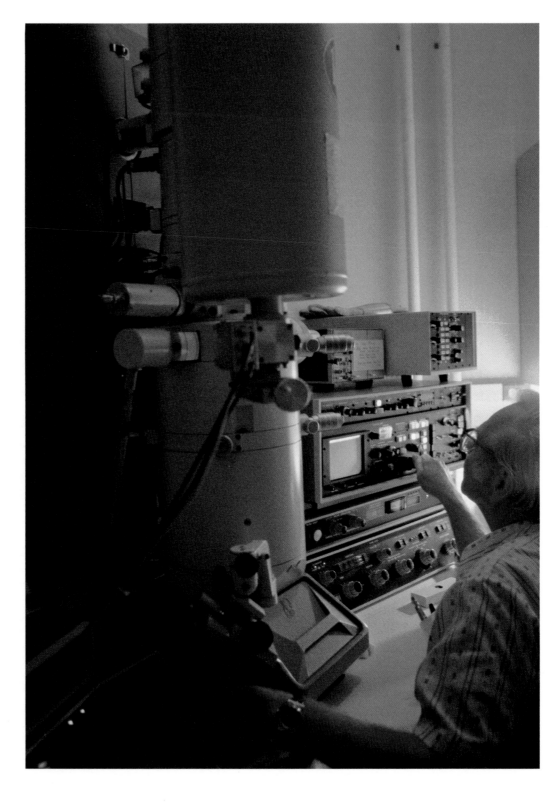

MARTIN MARIETTA

A high-technology company involved in the design, development and manufacture of major defense and space systems, Martin Marietta Aerospace employs approximately 2,500 in the Baltimore division. Here advanced systems engineering and precision manufacturing technology are employed, along with various materials in the production of a myriad of commercial and defense systems. It was here in Baltimore that the first missiles and space systems in the nation were developed. Among these were the Vanguard satellite launching vehicles and the Gemini-Titan boosters. Today's technology seems quite distant from some of the earlier creations of the Baltimore division — the famous China Clipper flying boat and the B-26 Marauder bomber.

First National Bank Of Maryland

FINANCIAL

Baltimore represents a major center of financial transactions for the southeastern region of the country. With changing trends throughout the years, various local institutions have flourished while others left the scene. Interestingly enough, as a number of financial institutions declined, the asset base of the remaining increased significantly.

Back in the early days of Baltimore, the port was the center of business life. Fortunes were made and lost as the result of successful and not-so-successful trading operations. One of the most successful was that begun by Alexander Brown, an immigrant from Ireland. Along with his sons, Brown financed large exports of cotton and other commodities to England and imports of European manufactured goods. To facilitate this operation, Brown made use of a fleet of sailing ships he acquired and bills of exchange that could be sold on the open market. Over the years the firm went into investment banking, and through innovation and adaptation has become one of the most respected names in the field throughout the world.

Baltimore has benefitted from individuals whose success resulted from banking. George Peabody, whose gift of more than $1 million established the Institute that bears his name, started a London company based upon banking principles. From the fortune he amassed, Peabody funded various projects in England and the American South. In addition, Baltimore acquired the Peabody Institute in Mount Vernon.

Another individual who profitted from various business activities including banking and investing, was Enoch Pratt. Baltimore benefitted in numerous ways from the love affair Pratt had with his adopted home. He gave $2 million to a good friend, Dr. Sheppard, for the creation of a hospital for the mentally ill, and he made an offer to the city fathers in which he promised some $833,333 for the creation of a library, as long as the city would support and maintain the facility with an annual contribution of $50,000. The mutual agreement created the Enoch Pratt Library system that serves the entire city today.

Finally, there is the success story that resulted in the creation of a major university and hospital. Through the successful venture that John Hopkins involved himself in, including banking and finance, he was able to endow various charities and the two institutions that bear his name.

Modern Baltimore is an active financial center. With increased and innovative services, banks, savings and loans, insurance companies and investment houses are today making products available that did not exist twenty years ago, ten years ago, or for that matter, one year ago. It is a competitive marketplace that, with deregulation taking place, suggests that activity in Baltimore will continue in a brisk atmosphere for years to come.

CENTRABANK

Begun in 1854 and first known as the Dime Savings Bank, CentraBank has had a unique history. Known by other names over the years, such as the Dime Savings Bank, Quaker Bank, and Central Savings Bank, CentraBank has its offices at the corners of North Charles and Lexington Streets in a building acquired in the 1979 merger with Arlington Federal Savings and Loan Association. Today CentraBank is responding to new demands made by better-informed consumers, offering such products as objective financial planning and special loan packages for computers. In a world of impersonal and totally-electronic banking, CentraBank is working to revive the concept of the "personal banker" with special need-based and outreach personnel and priority banking for special bank customers.

1ST NATIONAL BANK

The evolution of the First National Bank of Maryland began in 1806. When the Mechanics Bank of Baltimore opened its doors that year, it was one of only twenty-eight other banks in the entire country. It stood solid through depressions and panics, wars and natural disasters. It is interesting that the great fire of 1904, which literally destroyed the bank building, was unable to affect the huge vault that held the valuables of many local families. Mergers over the years have culminated in the creation of The First National Bank of Maryland as it exists today at 25 South Charles Street.

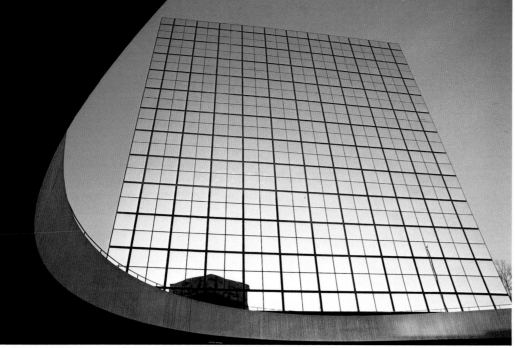

Blue Cross-Blue Shield

Monumental Life

O'Conor, Piper and Flynn

USF & G

O'CONOR, PIPER AND FLYNN

Five of Baltimore's best known real estate firms merged in 1984 to form a new entity, O'Conor, Piper and Flynn. The new firm is now the dominant, independent, locally owned and managed real estate company in the Baltimore area, with an annual sales volume of $735 million. Utilizing up to date marketing techniques and efficiency of a large corporation, it strives to keep a warm personal touch.

MONUMENTAL LIFE, USF & G, BLUE CROSS-BLUE SHIELD

Monumental Life Insurance Company has roots in Baltimore that go back to 1858, when it was started by George P. Kane.

The United States Fidelity & Guaranty Company has grown since 1896 to become one of the top multiple-line insurance companies in the nation.

Blue Cross and Blue Shield represents the largest health care and protection companies in the State of Maryland.

ALEX BROWN & SONS

The oldest name in investment banking in the United States, Alex Brown & Sons has held that distinction since its inception in 1800. Since it was founded, its growth has been based on strong capitalization, sound management, long-standing relationships, and the flexibility to meet changing conditions. Through good times and bad, the firm had distinguished itself from other American investment banking houses. The fine building that serves as its headquarters survived the devastation of the fire of 1904, when the rest of the busines center was destroyed. Today, it serves as nucleus for the firm's operations along the eastern seaboard.

Chesapeake Bay

SURROUNDING AREAS

Maryland is fortunate to have Baltimore and Baltimore is equally fortunate to be part of such a unique state.

As the Maryland Department of Tourism so aptly puts it, it is possible to "Capture a Maryland Memory." The areas that surround Baltimore are ripe with history and recreation, culture and entertainment, sports and the best eating. All the visitor has to do is reach out.

No matter where you travel, short day trips or long, overnight vacations, there is something around every curve in the road.

If history is an interest, the only problem is deciding where to begin. Both the Revolutionary and the Civil Wars were fought on Maryland soil and preserved on such fields of action as Fort Frederick and Antietam National Battlefield. In St. Mary's City a replica of The Dove can be seen at the dock where it brought some of Maryland's first settlers in 1634. In Cumberland, one can visit Washington's Headquarters used by the young lieutenant colonel in his early military career. And of course a stroll down any street in Annapolis is a step back in time.

Maryland is a state rich in recreational and sporting activities. Perhaps the most rugged of the offerings is whitewater rafting on the likes of the Savage River in Garrett County. However, there is also skiing, sailing, horseback riding, hiking, fishing and swimming in the crisp lakes or the Atlantic Ocean.

For those interested in good food and unique dining experiences, you cannot go wrong in Maryland. From steamed crabs to sour beef and dumplings, whatever the taste, it can be found across the state. Of course the bounty of the Chesapeake Bay and the rich production of local farmlands have gone hand-in-hand in making Maryland so popular.

As Maryland readies herself for a 350th birthday celebration in 1984, the future looks bright for the Free State. From the ancient Allegheny Mountains and majestic Chesapeake Bay, to the pounding surf of the Atlantic Ocean, Maryland is a unique place to live and work. From what many have seen, one of the oldest settled areas in the United States is just as young and vital as ever, with something to offer everyone.

ANNAPOLIS

A visitor to Annapolis can almost forget what century they are in. With its location on the Inland Waterway and with the capacity to provide berthing facilities for large numbers of pleasure craft, the entire area around the State Capital has continued to be an ever-popular tourist attraction. The United States Naval Academy, founded in 1845, is home to some of the finest examples of early American architecture to be found anywhere. It is interesting to note that the city has been Maryland's capital since 1694 and once was the capital of the United States from November of 1783 through August of 1784. Nearby, the huge twin spans of the Chesapeake Bay Bridge stand mute as thousands of travelers cross to the Eastern shore and thousands of craft of all sizes, both commercial and pleasure sail beneath.

ST. MARY'S

The counties of Southern Maryland are the oldest in the state. St. Mary's was first settled in 1634 when colonists arrived aboard the Ark and the Dove. Today a reconstruction of the first State House built in St. Mary's reflects just how far the colonists were able to come with their new venture in just 42 years. This has traditionally been tobacco country and the state's warehouses and loose-leaf auction houses are a hub of activity in the late Spring. Some 70 miles from Baltimore is the area around Charlotte Hall, where it is not unusual to see members of Maryland's Amish community traveling to and from their farms to the markets where their produce is sold. Just a little farther south are Calvert Cliffs, famous for the millions of Miocene period fossils that are so easily found.

Montgomery County

Washington D.C.

MONTGOMERY COUNTY, WASHINGTON, D.C.

Montgomery County represents one of the most affluent areas in the United States. With its proximity to the Nation's Capital, the region is an ever-growing area that has attracted science-oriented and clean sophisticated industry. With beautiful park-like settings and well-planned growth, Montgomery County has been a most popular area for the successful to live.

One of the chief attractions in the area is the C & O Canal Museum with its Crommelin House, which was built to attract visitors to the Great Falls and the scenic beauty of the Potomac River.

North Central

Columbia

NORTH CENTRAL MARYLAND

Just outside of Baltimore, are the placid and picturesque farmlands and pastures that mark the area of North Central Maryland. Today, the one-time dream of Baltimorean James Rouse has become a reality. Columbia stands as a testimonial to the concept of planned community life and to the foresight of an innovative and creative mind. Visitors to the area can sample home-grown fruits from roadside stands, stop by a working 19th century farm near Westminster, or travel back in time as they cross streams made passable by covered bridges. Much of this area is horse country and some of the finest animals in the nation have been raised on Maryland turf.

WESTERN MARYLAND

Traveling west from Cumberland, Maryland is a splendid variation of scenery and activity. Most of the commercial activity in the Western counties is centered around agriculture and tourism. With excellent recreational activities, from cross-country and downhill skiing to sailing the likes of Deep Creek Lake and backpacking along the Appalachian Trail, there is something for everyone in Western Maryland.

Ocean City

Eastern Shore

Eastern Shore

Ocean City

OCEAN CITY, EASTERN SHORE

Cross the Bay Bridge and enter another world within Maryland: the Eastern Shore. With names like Choptank and Wicomico, towns like St. Michael's and Oxford, and history intermingled with the daily lives of its residents, this is a place where past and present meet and life is not as fast paced. But listen and look again, because there is the far shore; there is Ocean City where surf and sand can make you almost forget the serenity just a few miles inland. Thousands gather each year to take advantage of spacious beaches and an atmosphere that is only to be found in Ocean City. It is only a short distance to Assateague Island where one can enjoy a unique, quiet beauty and see wild ponies roaming freely.

CORPORATE CREDITS

We would like to thank the following corporations for sponsorship (in terms of prepublication purchase of *Baltimore A Portrait*).

The Black & Decker Manufacturing Company
Baltimore Convention Bureau
First National Bank Of Maryland
Remington Book Stores
Maryland News Distributing Company
Greetings & Readings

Maryland Casualty Company
Baltimore Economic Development Corporation
B. Dalton Booksellers
CentraBank
Rossmann-Hurt-Hoffman, Inc. Insurance
Gordon's Booksellers

Maryland Port Administration
RTKL Associates Inc.
Phillips Seafood Restaurant
O'Conor, Piper and Flynn